THE EMBRACE OF BUILDINGS

THE EMBRACE OF BUILDINGS

A SECOND LOOK AT
WALKABLE CITY NEIGHBORHOODS

LEE HARDY

Calvin
COLLEGE
PRESS

GRAND RAPIDS, MICHIGAN

Published by
The Calvin College Press
3201 Burton Street SE
Grand Rapids, MI 49546
www.calvin.edu/press/

Cover and book design by Lee Hardy
Cover Illustration by Andrew von Maur, Bryce Buckley, Kevin Fresse,
and Lionel Johnson of Andrews University
Body text set in Warnock Pro regular 11/14. Warnock Pro was designed by Robert Slimbach in 2000 and named after John Warnock, the co-founder of Adobe Systems.

Printed in the United States of America

Library of Congress Cataloging-in-Publication Data
Hardy, Lee, author.
The Embrace of Buildings: a second look at walkable city neighborhoods / Lee Hardy.
Includes bibliographic references and index.
Grand Rapids, MI: Calvin College Press, 2017.
ISBN 978-1-937555-25-2 (pbk.)
ISBN 978-1-937555-26-9 (ebook)
1. LCSH City Traffic—Planning. 2. Streets—Planning. 3. Pedestrian areas.
4. Transportation, Automotive. 5. Roads—Design and construction. 6. Transit oriented development. 7. Sustainable urban development. 8. Community development, urban. 9. Segregation. 10. Vocation—Christianity. 11. Cities and towns—Religious aspects—Christianity. 12. Human ecology—Religious aspects—Christianity. 13. BISAC ARCHITECTURE/Urban and Land Use Planning. 14. Architecture/Sustainability and Green Design.

LCC HE305 H37 2017
DDC 725.3—dc23

"Above all, do not lose your desire to walk. Every day I walk myself into a state of well-being and walk away from every illness. I have walked myself into my best thoughts, and I know of no thought so burdensome that one cannot walk away from it."

Søren Kierkegaard

Contents

Preface

MY FLIGHT was scheduled to arrive at LAX at 11:30 in the morning. Perfect, I thought. I could get a rental car and be out of Los Angeles before rush hour, heading up the California coast to visit my father by mid-afternoon. But my plans were spoiled by a thunderstorm in Chicago, which added five hours to my travel time. I arrived in LA at 4:30, picked up the rental car, and quickly got on the 405 northbound. It then took me one hour to go eight miles. And there were miles of heavy traffic still in front of me. Exasperated, I imagined an aerial view of my situation: surrounded by hundreds of cars on an expressway that now looked more like a linear parking lot. Clearly something was wrong with that picture.

Since my ill-timed visit, the 405 underwent a $1.6 billion construction project to ease traffic by expanding its capacity. After adding a travel lane and a set of new on- and off-ramps, the results are in: according to a study of the LA County Metropolitan Transportation Authority, the 405 is now even more congested between the hours of 4:30 and

6:30 pm.[1] The results could have been predicted. Adding capacity to highways rarely reduces traffic congestion. It just invites more drivers. The phenomenon is known as "induced traffic." We have known about it for years. And yet we keep spending tax dollars on the same old solutions, which often just make things worse.

I am a philosopher by training. But I present to you a book on urban design. Much of the content of this book is drawn from an interim course on urbanism I've been teaching for the last ten years at Calvin College in Grand Rapids, Michigan.

When people ask me how I got interested in urban issues, my short answer is: "I grew up in LA." My long answer is that I grew up in Fullerton, in Orange County, about thirty-five miles southeast of LA, during the 1960s. At the beginning of that decade, Orange County was a collection of distinct towns surrounded by orange groves and bean fields. My father owned a drugstore on Harbor Boulevard, the main street of Fullerton, which would take you to Newport Beach after a half-hour drive to the south. As a child I performed a variety of menial jobs in the store, often pausing to listen to conversations my father held with his regular customers, who also seemed like his friends. Lives were shared; local affairs discussed. Later I supplemented my income by filling in for my friends who delivered *The Fullerton News-Tribune*, the local paper, on the east side of town.

By the mid-1960s, the character of the region was changing rapidly. A carpet of housing subdivisions, shopping malls, parking lots, freeways, and gas stations was being rolled out from LA. Soon the orange groves and bean fields disappeared, and Orange County became one vast undifferentiated conurbation. It was difficult to tell when you left one town and entered another. The towns themselves had been gutted as retail moved out to the malls. Typical travel distances lengthened, and traffic became a serious problem. *The Fullerton News-Tribune* folded and became a weekly section of *The Orange County Register.* When asked by outsiders where they lived, people rarely named their town anymore. They just said, "Orange County." It didn't seem to matter where you lived, as long as you were reasonably close to a highway and the TV reception was good. At the end of his career, my father worked for a chain drugstore in a supermarket far removed from his place of residence. His customers were strangers to him, and remained so. Just about all traces of civic life and identity, it seemed, had evaporated.

The pattern of post-World War II development I witnessed in Orange County struck me as fundamentally wrong-headed. But others appeared to accept it as inevitable and somehow normal. I found few people voicing concerns. Until, in September of 1996, I read an article in *The Atlantic Monthly* by James Howard Kuntsler.[2] The article was drawn from his earlier book, *The Geography of Nowhere*, and previewed his forthcoming book entitled *Home from Nowhere.* In that piece, Kunstler articulated all the private feelings I had been harboring about urban sprawl, often in sustained and delightful runs of purple prose. Underneath his impassioned writing style, however, lay a solid analysis of the effects and drawbacks of functional zoning and automobile dependence. Following up on that lead, I soon discovered the existence of the Congress for the New Urbanism, an organization of architects, city planners, and citizen activists devoted to the retrieval of classic urban form and the creation of walkable city neighborhoods. I joined the Congress and attended many of its national conferences. I delved into the literature on urban design and the cultural history of cities. I did coursework at the University of Miami School of Architecture. I studied cities as I traveled in North America, Europe, and Asia. I made contacts with like-minded architects, planners, and developers in the Grand Rapids area, and then began to offer a course on urban design during the January interim at Calvin College.

The New Urbanist movement was controversial when it came together in the mid-1990s. But its sentiments, it seemed to me, were little more than a straightforward extension of common sense. Consider the opening statement of its Charter, adopted in 1996: "The Congress for the New Urbanism views disinvestment in central cities, the spread of placeless sprawl, increasing separation by race and income, environmental deterioration, loss of agricultural lands and wilderness, and the erosion of society's built heritage as one interrelated community-building challenge."[3] Clearly the problems identified by the Congress were genuine problems. Or so I thought. Its agenda also seemed to me to be on the right track: "We stand for the restoration of existing urban centers and towns within coherent metropolitan regions, the reconfiguration of sprawling suburbs into communities of real neighborhoods and diverse districts, the conservation of natural environments, and the preservation of our built legacy." Moreover, the recommended means and guidelines appeared well-fitted to its proposed ends: "We advocate the restructuring of public policy and development practices to support the following principles: neighborhoods should be diverse in use and population; communities should be designed for the pedestrian and transit as well as the car; cities and towns should be shaped by physically defined and universally accessible public spaces and community institutions; urban places should be framed by architecture and landscape design that celebrate local history, climate, ecology, and building practice." I could find much to affirm and little to argue with in the Charter.

Nevertheless, the New Urbanism has had its share of critics. Some hold that it subscribes to a version of "architectural determinism," as if getting the physical form of cities right would somehow guarantee a well-functioning human community. I have yet to meet a new urbanist who holds such a view. In fact, this objection is anticipated in the fourth paragraph of the Charter: "We recognize that physical solutions by themselves will not solve social and economic problems, but neither can economic vitality, community stability, and environmental health be sustained without a coherent and supportive physical framework." Good urban form is best thought of as an enabling condition, not an all-determining factor.

Others have criticized New Urbanism because many new developments built along its principles occupy higher price points in the real estate market. They tend to be exclusive and unaffordable. The high prices, however, reflect the level of demand for such places. They are indeed attractive. And rare. The solution to that problem is to build more of them, not less.

New Urbanism has also been criticized as a pointless exercise in nostalgia, a futile attempt to turn back the clock to the quaint towns and neighborhoods of yesteryear, when in fact the future marches on, inexorably, to bold new experiments in oddly shaped glass towers, massive superhighways, and electronically assisted automotive transportation. In response to this claim, I can only point out that what comes later in time does not always represent true progress. As C. S. Lewis reminded us in *Mere Christianity*, "We all want progress. But progress means getting nearer to the place where you want to be. And if you have taken a wrong turning, then to go forward does not get you any nearer. If you are on the wrong road, progress means doing an about-turn and walking back to the right road; and in that case the man who turns back soonest is the most progressive man."[4] In the body of this book, I argue that low density, auto-oriented development is in fact taking us down the wrong road, and that turning back to rediscover the principles of classic urban form represents a step in the right direction.

Finally, it has often been said that New Urbanism is doomed to failure because it will never get Americans to abandon their cars. But that was never the aim of the movement in the first place. The point is to promote the creation of places where driving remains an option, but is not a necessity, places where alternate modes of transit are available. The addition of transit options not only serves the one third of Americans who do not—or cannot—drive; it also makes it possible for some households to reduce the number of cars they must own, thus saving thousands of dollars a year.

My interest in walkable city neighborhoods is not merely theoretical. It's also part of my experience. I have lived in such a neighborhood in Grand Rapids for the past thirty years. It goes by the name of Eastown. It's an old streetcar suburb that was largely built out in the 1910s, before car ownership was widespread. People, primarily professionals in that day, would take the streetcar downtown to work, return, and walk home. Home may have been a single-family detached house. Or it may have been a duplex or apartment. Eastown contains a variety of residential options. The neighborhood had its own retail section that supplied residents with their daily and weekly needs within a comfortable walking distance.

Much has changed since then. A good number of buildings have been lost to parking lots. Some of the retail has moved out to big box stores on the edge of the city. But the community still has good bone structure, a fine network of connected streets. And many walkable destinations. Within a five-minute walk of my house lies a farmer's market, a supermarket, three churches, two elementary schools, a civic theater, two coffee shops, a pizza parlor, a donut shop, three restaurants, two bakeries, a brewery, a park, a college, a creek, two used book stores, a shoe store, a yoga studio, a massage therapist, two beauty salons, a gift shop, a gym, a butcher shop, a delicatessen, a post office, a bike shop, and a bus stop. My wife and I make do with one car, since I can ride my bike or moped to work in fair weather and take the bus in foul.

Our four children, now grown, have fond memories of living in a neighborhood where they could walk to the park and its playground, to the supermarket for candy, or to the coffee shop for hot chocolate with their friends. They grew up in a house where the front porch was just eight feet back from the sidewalk, and the neighbors' houses were just eleven feet to each side. In the summers the doors of the houses on our block were open, and they and their friends easily circulated from house to house and yard to yard under the welcoming and watchful eye of their adult neighbors. Once a year we close the street for a block party. Then not only the food but also the musical instruments come out, and the fire department often supplies a big red fire engine for the children to inspect. In the summers, on random Friday afternoons, someone will announce a spontaneous Happy Hour, and we'll gather on a porch for drinks and hors d'oeuvres. Every December we go caroling with a group of about a dozen neighbors. Those among us who fall ill can expect visits and regular deliveries of prepared food. We have made many friends in our part of town, and many acquaintances. The built form of our neighborhood did not make us sociable; but it made it easier for us to be social.

The aim of this book is to provide the reader with a manageable overview of key issues connected with three forms of human settlement—urban, suburban, and exurban—as they have come to expression in North America. Along the way, I will point out some of the forgotten virtues of urban neighborhoods, and some of the problems now associated with suburban and especially exurban development. It is best to think of the chapters of this book as a series of mini-essays on topics that deserve—and have received—more detailed treatment elsewhere. At the end of the book I suggest resources in print and on the web for those who wish to pursue those topics.

I have many to thank for their assistance in the development of this book. First, to those who read and commented upon earlier versions of the manuscript: Jay Hoekstra, Eric

Jacobsen, Christopher Miller, Mark Bjelland, Mark Mulder, Jamie Smith, Matt Halteman, Jonathan Bradford, Jon Ippel, Cory Willson, John Terpstra, Chris Elisara, and my wife, Judith Hardy, an editor by trade and trustworthy advisor by nature. Second, to Robert B. Krushwitz, editor of *Christian Reflection*, for permission to use a revised version of an article I published in that journal for the first four chapters of this book. Third, to the Calvin College Alumni Association for a grant to travel to Amsterdam and Copenhagen to study the urban bike infrastructure of those fine cities. Fourth, to my son Ian Hardy, a reference librarian with formidable IT skills who helped me track down needed government data. Fifth, to Andrew von Maur, professor of architecture in the urban design program of Andrews University, for permission to use on the cover of this book the watercolor representation of the proposed Grand Rapids Fisher's Station development he created along with three architecture students, Bryce Buckley, Kevin Fresse, and Lionel Johnson. Finally, to Susan Felch, editor of the Calvin College Press, for first suggesting that I write a book on this topic; to Lisa Early, copy editor for the press; to Dale Williams and Steve Kline for help in production; and to the Henry Institute and the Institute of Christian Worship at Calvin College for financial support in publication.

I should mention that I have created a free illustrated companion to this book, available at www.calvin.edu/press. Readers can go to this website to scroll through the visuals that display the concepts, places, and references in the book, page by page, chapter by chapter. The ideal way to read this book is with a laptop or tablet at hand.

Notes

1. "Los Angeles Drivers Ask: Was $1.6 Billion Worth It?," *The New York Times* (December 20, 2016): A12 .

2. James Howard Kunstler, "Home from Nowhere," *The Atlantic Monthly,* 278, no. 3 (September, 1996): 43-66.

3. See cnu.org/charter

4. C. S. Lewis, *Mere Christianity* (New York: HarperCollins, 2001), 28.

Chapter 1

The Invisible Hand of Uncle Sam

IN 1990, I SPENT a sabbatical year with my family in the German city of Cologne. Despite all the things that make living in a foreign country difficult, it was for us a year of unalloyed urban joy. We did not own a car. But that didn't matter in the least. I rode a bike to the university. The church we attended was just a four-block walk from our apartment. The elementary school my children went to was also close by and required no bus. The main street of our neighborhood, three blocks away, offered all we needed on a daily basis—a grocery store, a bakery, a flower shop, a newsstand, a stationery store, two bookstores, and several restaurants. The *Stadtwald*—a ten-mile long park that rings the western edge of the city—was just a ten-minute walk along a pleasant canal, putting playgrounds, tennis courts, tearooms, lakes with boat rentals, and, most importantly, ice-cream vendors within our family's pedestrian reach. On weekends we often took the bus downtown. On the plaza before the great Cologne cathedral there was always something free and festive going on—church choirs, street musicians, sidewalk artists, magicians, mimes, and acrobats. On top of that, there were no neighborhoods to avoid. There were no crime-ridden slums. German society may have its share of problems, but putting together humane, coherent, and delightful cities is not one of them.

How painful to return home and be reminded of the sorry state of the urban fabric in North America. So many of our inner cities have been abandoned, converted into deadzones, warehouses for those too poor to leave, their streets mean and shabby, their buildings vandalized, their stores boarded up, their schools closed, permeated by an atmosphere of fear and despair. As a member of the American middle class, of course, I didn't have to deal with those urban realities. I was to return to my home on the outskirts of town, often driving where I needed to go along gritty commercial thoroughfares and featureless arterials, past junky strip malls, gas stations, big box retail, fast food joints, and cartoon signage, hunting for advantageous parking spots in paved lots large enough to accommodate an entire European village. Granted, our four-bedroom, single-family detached house was nice, easily larger than any German family's we knew. Most of them lived in apartments. Our society excels when it comes to private space. But why have we in America given up on public space, both urban and suburban? Must we choose between deteriorating urban cores and degraded suburban landscapes? Where did we go wrong?

It is tempting to think that the current reality of our built environment is the simple result of pristine market forces. But such is not the case. Since the 1930s, the federal government has skewed the housing market in favor of suburban home construction.[1] In an effort to prevent foreclosures on homes during the Depression, the Roosevelt administration created the Home Owners Loan Corporation in 1933, which refinanced over a million short-term home mortgages with fully amortized mortgages stretched over fifteen to twenty-five years. In the year following, President Roosevelt signed the National Housing Act, thus creating the FHA (Federal Housing Administration). The FHA was designed to stimulate the housing market by insuring long-term, low-interest private home mortgages. In many cases, these mortgages made purchasing a home cheaper than renting.[2] But the FHA was not about to insure mortgages indiscriminately. It had guidelines. And those guidelines clearly favored single-family homes of recent construction. The FHA did not back generous, long-term loans for the repair of existing homes. Nor was it interested in supporting the construction of multi-family units. Nor did it smile upon classic urban row housing. Even for the construction of new single-family houses, it had definite ideas, specifying suburban lot sizes and set-backs for any home it would consider an ideal candidate for an insured mortgage. And the home industry built accordingly—especially after the Second War World when the 1944 GI Bill of Rights authorized the Veterans Administration to guarantee zero down payment home loans for sixteen million returning GIs. The suburban boom was off to a resounding start.

New Deal measures for putting the economy back on track not only shaped the style of American post-war residential stock, it also promoted social separation by race, class, and ethnicity in the name of sound investment. The Home Owners Loan Corporation rated residential areas for risk at four levels, color-coded on secret "Residential Security Maps" in green, blue, yellow, and red. The highest

rating (green) was given to newly constructed neighborhoods populated by white middle-class professionals. If such
residential areas were "infiltrated by Jews," they were auto-
matically dropped down to the next rating tier. The worst
rating (red) was invariably given to black neighborhoods,
making it unlikely that anyone could obtain a low-interest,
federally insured home loan there—hence the term "redlining." Shunned by the banks, most African-American families
had to settle for rental units run by absentee landlords. Those
looking to own a home had few places to turn but to often
predatory land contracts, which combined all the responsibilities of home ownership with all the vulnerabilities
of renting. Miss one monthly payment, and you could be
summarily evicted with zero equity. In the mid-1960's, 85
percent of the homes bought by African Americans were
on land contracts.[3]

In its appraisal system for determining housing value,
the FHA downgraded traditional urban neighborhoods that
were old, dense, and contained non-residential elements
such as offices and retail establishments. It also downgraded
neighborhoods harboring "inharmonious racial or nationality groups."[4] Until 1948, its Underwriting Manual advocated
the use of restrictive covenants, written into property deeds,
prohibiting the sale of homes in predominately white neighborhoods to black families.[5] The real estate industry pitched
in as well. The 1924 "Code of Ethics" for the National Association of Real Estate Boards stated that "A Realtor should
never be instrumental in introducing to a neighborhood a
character of property or occupancy, members of any race or
nationality, or any individual whose presence will be clearly
detrimental to property values in a neighborhood."[6] I think

we all understand which races were considered "detrimental to property values."

The FHA guaranteed low-interest loans not only for individual home buyers. It also pre-approved homes in an entire subdivision, provided they were built according to its specifications. Such homes, already approved for FHA guaranteed loans to qualified homebuyers, did not require an additional appraisal. That made them easier to sell. Developers wishing for FHA approval before going to the banks for a low-interest loan had to meet certain requirements specifying the zoning regulations, materials, and design for the homes in their proposed subdivision. More often than not, however, there was one other requirement: not to sell the homes to African-Americans.[7] In fact, the FHA not only did not want African-Americans in the subdivisions it sponsored, it didn't even want them near the subdivisions it sponsored. If African-American neighborhoods were in the vicinity, the FHA favored sites separated from those neighborhoods by "natural or artificial barriers."[8] When in 1940 a developer on the north side of Detroit was refused FHA approval because of the proximity of a predominantly black neighborhood to his proposed subdivision, he built a wall a half mile long, six feet high, and one foot thick on the edge of his property—his artificial barrier. He then received the green light from the FHA. The wall still stands today, just south of Eight Mile Road.

The proximity of white and black neighborhoods led to another practice in the real estate industry that often worked hand-in-hand with redlining to reinforce housing segregation. It was called "blockbusting." Looking to buy low and sell high, real estate agents were known to send signals throughout white neighborhoods of an impending "negro invasion." The tactics varied. Sometimes African-American women were paid to stroll through bordering white neighborhoods with baby carriages; sometimes African-American men were hired to drive through the neighborhood with the windows rolled down, soul music blaring; sometimes real estate agents would go door-to-door, asking if homes were for sale, accompanied by an African-American. Once white homeowners were panicked into selling their homes at bargain basement prices, the real estate agents would buy them and then turn around and sell them to middle-class African-American families, who would pay premium prices for the few homes available to them. But once the process started and the neighborhood was integrated, the FHA would redline the neighborhood for harboring "inharmonious racial groups." White homebuyers would then look elsewhere, in the distant suburbs, for FHA-friendly homes. The neighborhood would be integrated for only a short time before it was segregated once again. This time, all black.[9]

Federal housing policies in combination with widespread racial animosities virtually guaranteed that the largely white middle class would abandon urban neighborhoods for the suburbs—and that black families would not follow them. They promoted socially segregated middle-class residential neighborhoods exclusively made up of detached single-family homes. And that's what we got.

Notes

1. Here I follow Kenneth Jackson's account of American suburbanization in his classic study, *Crabgrass Frontier: The Suburbanization of the United States* (New York: Oxford University Press, 1985), 190-218.

2. In 1938, the National Housing Act was amended to set up the Federal National Mortgage Association, also known as "Fannie Mae," which was authorized to buy FHA-insured home mortgages from local lenders. Creating a secondary mortgage market would provide additional stimulus to the housing industry by supplying local lenders with more capital that could in turn be plowed back into additional home loans. This move on the part of the federal government set up the conditions for the international system of mortgage finance, and mortgage-backed securities, we know today. After the Clinton administration pushed Fannie Mae to increase its portfolio of sub-prime mortgages to lower-income households, it also laid the groundwork for the sub-prime mortgage crisis and the Great Recession of 2008-2012. See Brian J. McCabe, *No Place Like Home: Wealth, Community and the Politics of Homeownership* (Oxford: Oxford University Press, 2016), 52; and Steven A. Holmes, "Fannie Mae Eases Credit to Aid Mortgage Lending," *The New York Times*, September 30, 1999, http://www.nytimes.com/1999/09/30/business/fannie-mae-eases-credit-to-aid-mortgage-lending.html.

3. Richard Rothstein, *The Color of Law: a Forgotten History of How Our Government Segregated America* (New York: Liverlight Publishing Company, 2017), 98. In land contracts, the home buyer purchases the house directly from the home owner with no bank involved. The title remains with the home owner until the last payment is made on the house. Typically the last payment is a "balloon payment" because the monthly payments, taken together, do not cover the entire amount of the principle.

4. Jackson, *Crabgrass Frontier*, 208.

5. Jackson, *Crabgrass Frontier*, 209.

6. Quoted in Todd E. Robinson, *A City within a City: The Black Freedom Struggle in Grand Rapids, Michigan* (Philadelphia: Temple University Press, 2013), 74.

7. Rothstein, *Color of Law*, 71.

8. Rothstein, *Color of Law*, 65.

9. Rothstein, *Color of Law*, 12-13, 95.

Chapter 2

In Every Garage a Car—
No, Make That Two Cars

W E ASSOCIATE the suburbs not only with low density single-family residential development but also with the exclusive reliance on the private automobile for transportation. Again, wc might think that the relative lack of public transportation in vast reaches of our built environment is the simple result of pristine market forces. But again we would be mistaken. Our disproportionate use of the car has been encouraged by federal spending priorities since the Second World War, along with some very clever market strategies on the part of the automobile industry.

Cars need good roads if they are to be an attractive transportation option. Automobile manufacturers would be happy to supply the cars, if only the government would supply car-worthy roads. In the 1920s, America's national road system was not in good repair. Paved highways were few and far between. Most Americans traveled long distances by rail; 250,000 miles of heavy rail were in use across the nation. Extensive inter-urban lines served regional travel needs. And within the cities, electric streetcars were the principal form of conveyance. At the time, American public transportation was second to none. During the Depression era of the 1930s, however, FDR had already envisioned a federal job-making project of constructing six interstate highways, three running north to south, three running east to west. A version of that project was aggressively marketed by General Motors in its stunning *Futurama* exhibit at the 1939 New York World's Fair, designed to sell America on the glorious vision of a nation crisscrossed by fourteen-lane, limited access super-highways. At the close of the Second World War, the project was bumped up the federal priority list, given the imminent need to employ millions of returning GIs.

Funding, however, was a problem. When Dwight Eisenhower came into office, an advisory committee on a national highway system was formed. Eisenhower appointed his war colleague, the retired general Lucius D. Clay, to head the committee. Clay, as it turned out, was also a member of the board of directors for General Motors. He was joining familiar company in the executive branch: Charles Wilson, former CEO of General Motors, was then the Secretary of Defense. It should come as no surprise that the committee found effective means of financing the interstate highway project. The federal government would pay for 90 percent of it through a hidden gas tax. In 1956, Eisenhower signed the National System of Interstate and Defense Highways Act, authorizing the construction of 41,000 miles of roadway, the largest peacetime public works project in the history of the world. Soon after, 1,795 miles were added. Today the interstate highway system spans 46,876 miles.[1]

In the meantime, while Europe was wisely rebuilding its passenger rail systems, our rail systems received little support. In fact, they had been under attack for some time. In 1921, Alfred P. Sloan, then president of General Motors, had become convinced that the automobile market was already saturated. Sales were stagnating. Although only one in nine American households owned a car at that point, demand was limited by the extensive use of electric railway systems that served our nation's cities. In 1922, Sloan formed a special task force within GM dedicated to replacing the local and regional passenger railways with cars, trucks, and buses. By 1936, GM had acquired New York Railways and then ran it into the ground. In the same year it formed, together with Firestone Tire, Phillips Petroleum, and Standard Oil, National City Lines, a holding company that proceeded to acquire and then dismantle one hundred urban rail systems in forty-five cities across the country. In 1949, GM was found guilty of criminal conspiracy for its actions by a U. S. District Court in Chicago—and fined a token $5,000. Its executives were fined the grand sum of $1.00 each.[2]

The dramatic downgrading of our public transportation systems, together with the construction of the interstate highway system, did much to fuel the suburban boom of the 1960s. The highways opened up relatively inexpensive rural land for the development of housing subdivisions. One could now live in the country and commute to work in the city by car. That boom turned into a massive explosion in the 1970s when combined with two other factors: strict functional zoning and the street hierarchy. Both of those factors have their roots in the early twentieth century.

Zoning ordinances grant municipal and county governments the power to abridge the property rights of some to protect the health, wellbeing, and property values of others.

We can't just do or build anything we like on the land that we own. There are limitations. Functional zoning codes specify those limitations by land use: commercial, office, civic, residential, industrial, and the like. If, for example, an area is zoned for residential, then no commercial buildings will be built there; if zoned for commercial, then no residential buildings are allowed. First invoked by New York City in 1916, then promulgated in a model code developed by the federal government under the direction of then Secretary of Commerce Herbert Hoover, and later supported by a Supreme Court decision in 1926 (*Euclid v. Ambler*), zoning codes were in wide use in most localities by the late 1920s.

Initially, land use restrictions were employed to keep heavy industry out of residential areas, which makes perfect sense. Since then, however, they've gone to the extreme. Not only is heavy industry separated from residential, but light industry, commercial, office, and civic land uses are as well. In addition, modern zoning ordinances often separate residential areas according to different residential types (single-family houses, condominiums, multi-family apartment buildings, and so on). Even areas zoned for single-family houses will be separated by lot sizes—two-acre lots here, one-acre lots there, and half-acre lots somewhere else. Until recently it was illegal in most places to build an apartment over a retail establishment, a duplex next to an office, or even a duplex next to a single-family home. Mixed use is taboo.

Since the various land uses are now separated into distant and distinct land use areas or "pods," as they are called, it is no longer feasible to get between them by walking. We have to use the car. This is where the street hierarchy comes in. Conceived by the German architect Ludwig Hilberseimer in the 1920s, and imported to the States when he moved to Chicago in 1938 and took up a teaching post in city planning at the Illinois Institute of Technology, the street hierarchy was intended to prevent automobile through-traffic in developed areas.[3] Rather than laying streets out in a grid pattern—with variations, of course—the street hierarchy envisions a system of major arterials flowing between discrete land use pods. The pods themselves were to be serviced by cul-de-sacs that empty into collector roads that in turn empty into the major arterials. Dendritic in plan, the street hierarchy resembles the root system of a tree.

The suburbs of the 1950s and 1960s were usually laid out on a version of the grid pattern. They allowed for some embedded civic land uses such as churches and schools, and they were oriented to the center of town as a place of employment, entertainment, and administration. Since the 1970s, however, we have embarked on a historically unprecedented form of human settlement: the "exburb," centerless sprawl that has made the private automobile the only viable mode of transportation, where various land uses—residential, commercial, office, civic, and industrial—are strictly segregated and scattered across the countryside, and where most commutes are no longer between edge and center, but from edge to edge. If there is any center to this system, it is the home—where all trips originate and to which they return. That is to say, there are many centers, and they are all private. Exurban residents, as geographer Justin Wilford points out, now assemble their own personal urban environments out of disparate destinations within a drivable range of their domicile.[4] Shared public space—built, formed, used, and valued—has virtually disappeared.

14 THE EMBRACE OF BUILDINGS

Notes

1. See fhwa.dot.gov/interstate/faq.cfm.

2. For the story of National City Lines, see Jane Holtz Kay, *Asphalt Nation: How the Automobile Took Over America, and How We Can Take It Back* (Berkeley: University of California, 1997), 231-33; Kenneth Jackson, *The Crabgrass Frontier: the Suburbanization of the United States* (New York: Oxford University Press, 1985), 249-50; James Howard Kunstler, *The Geography of Nowhere* (New York: Touchstone, 1993), 106-8; and Bradford Snell, U. S. Counsel, "American Ground Transport," in Part 4A of Hearings in S. 1167, the Industrial Reorganization Act, before the Subcommittee on Antitrust and Monopoly of the Committee of the Judiciary, U.S. Senate, 93rd Congress, 2nd Session (Washington, DC, 1974).

3. Ludwig Hilberseimer, *The New City: Principles of Planning*, (Chicago: Paul Theobald, 1944), 104-7. To be fair, Hilberseimer insisted that residents in the kind of "settlement unit" he had in mind should be able to walk to work and that their children should be able to walk to school. No doubt he would be horrified to learn of the way his street hierarchy was detached from the discipline of more comprehensive planning and applied at random in our exurban regions.

4. Justin Wilford, *Sacred Subdivisions* (New York: New York University Press, 2012), 66.

Chapter 3

Every Home a Country Villa

T HE TECHNICAL MEANS of transportation, land development, and road building have made the exurb possible.
But the exurb became probable only with the push of a cultural ideal that valued the private domestic sphere over the
public realm of the city. In the Anglo-American tradition,
that ideal had its birth in England during the industrial age
of the nineteenth century. Prior to the Industrial Revolution, most middling families of professionals, artisans, and
merchants lived in city centers. And for many, work and
home were combined in the same building. As the merchants
benefited from the wealth generated by industrialization, and
as that same process filled the cities with smoke, grime, and
hordes of working class people, the most fortunate members of the bourgeoisie built country villas outside of town
as weekend retreats for the family. There they emulated
the life of the landed gentry even if they didn't make their
money from land rents. Eventually families were moved
out to the country villa full-time, and the male head of the
household commuted by carriage into the city for work. Thus
was home-life and work-life divided between the private

domestic sphere of the family in the country, managed by the female, and the public sphere of work in the city, run by the male. In the 1820s, English architect John Nash came up with the idea of building country-like villas in park-like yards next to rural-like curvilinear streets on the eastern edge of Regent's Park in London. Behold: the suburban formula was struck. The story of the growth of suburbia is the story of the gradual democratization of this arrangement, made possible by increasingly affordable homes and transportation. The entire middle class, and a good deal of the working class, could now live in downsized versions of the country villa on the edge of town in a naturalistic setting provided by a private yard. Every man a duke over his own domain.[1]

For the Anglo-evangelical community, the move to the suburbs was not only a privilege afforded by wealth. It was also a religious duty. William Wilberforce, a leading British evangelical of the Victorian period, is rightly remembered and revered for his central role in the abolition of slave trade in the British Empire. But he was equally dedicated to what he called the "reformation of manners." To that end he advised Christian families to remove themselves from the corrupting influence of the cities and devote themselves to the nurture of religious virtue within the suburban enclosure of the home. The religious valuation of city and suburb received a gender overlay as well: men, morally compromised by their involvement in the dog-eat-dog world of the city, were to have their "languid piety" revived at home by their wives, who, Wilberforce maintained, are "naturally more disposed to Religion than men."[2]

The suburban ideal, together with its religious interpretation, was imported to the States in the mid-nineteenth

century by Catherine Beecher and Andrew Jackson Downing. While her sister's book, *Uncle Tom's Cabin* (1852),
advanced Wilberforce's anti-slavery agenda, Catherine
Beecher's own work, *Treatise on Domestic Economy* (1841),
vigorously promoted the reformation of manners. And it
did so by way of the same cultural strategy: the home, as a
source of Christian morality, was to be physically separated
from the evil influences of the city. Author of *The Architecture of Country Houses* (1850), Downing too believed
"above all things under Heaven, in the power and influence
of the individual home."[3] A cottage in a picturesque setting
"all breathe forth to us, in true earnest tones, a domestic
feeling that at once purifies the heart and binds us closer to
our fellow beings."[4]

The domestic ideology of Beecher and Downing represents a dramatic relocation of the appropriate site of
human flourishing from the public realm of the city to the
private domain of the home. Yale urban historian Delores
Hayden deftly notes this shift in cultural ideals: "The dream
house is a uniquely American form. For the first time in
history, a civilization has created a utopian ideal based on
the house rather than the city or nation. For hundreds of
years, when individuals thought about putting an end to
social problems, they designed model towns to express
these desires, not model homes."[5] Governor John Winthrop,
leading a group of English Calvinists to America in 1630,
intended to establish the godly community as a shining "city
on a hill," a light to the nations. Now, it seems, we'll settle
for a house with a yard and the porch light on.

The pivot to the private in the nineteenth century was
entirely in keeping with the development of democratic

culture in America. In 1831, the Frenchman Alexis de Tocqueville visited the United States. Coming from old Europe
and its aristocratic ways, he took himself to be peering into
the future of Western society. In the record of his obser-
vations, *Democracy in America*, he spoke of the spirit of
American individualism. By that term he did not mean that
Americans were especially selfish. Far from it. He meant
rather that the center of American concern was the well-
being of the family, not society at large. "'Individualism,'"
he wrote, "is a word recently coined to express a new idea.
Our fathers only knew about egoism. Egoism is a passionate
and exaggerated love of self which leads a man to think of
all things in terms of himself and to prefer himself to all.
Individualism is a calm and considered feeling which dis-
poses each citizen to isolate himself from the mass of his
fellows and withdraw into the circle of family and friends;
with this little society formed to his taste, he gladly leaves
the greater society to look after itself."[6] In the democratic
culture Americans had invented for themselves, private
life outranks public life. The American suburb, as we now
know it, is the entirely predictable physical expression of
that spirit.[7]

However pervasive the spirit of American individualism
might be, however noble its emphasis on self-reliance, however laudable the amount of attention it devotes to the family,
de Tocqueville was convinced it represented a serious error
in judgment. What this spirit fails to recognize is the degree
to which the welfare of the private domain depends upon
the quality of the public realm. The fate of the family is in
fact wrapped up in the good fortunes of the city. When an
issue of common concern comes up, it sometimes happens

that "each man notices that he is not as independent of his fellows as he used to suppose."[8] Yet,

> It is difficult to force a man out of himself and get him to take an interest in the affairs of the whole state, for he has little understanding of the way in which the fate of the state can influence his own lot. But if it is a question of taking a road past his property, he sees at once that this small public matter has a bearing on his greatest private interests, and there is no need to point out to him the close connection between his private profit and the general interest.[9]

We like to think of ourselves as self-sufficient individuals. But we are in fact interdependent members of a larger whole. Much of our own good is inextricably bound up with the common good. De Tocqueville sought to remind us of this humbling reality. But he wasn't the first. In the pages of *Democracy in America* one can hear echoes of the Old Testament prophet Jeremiah. Addressing himself to the Jews in their Babylonian captivity, he admonishes them to "seek the welfare of the city where I have sent you into exile, and pray to the Lord on its behalf, for in its welfare you will find your welfare" (Jeremiah 29:7).

Notes

1. See Robert Fishman, *Bourgeois Utopias: The Rise and Fall of Suburbia* (New York: Basic Books, 1987), 18-102.

2. William Wilberforce, *A Practical View of the Prevailing Religious System of Professed Christians, in the Higher and Middle Classes of this Country, Contrasted with Real Christianity*, 11th ed. (London: Cadell and Davies, 1815), 365.

3. Andrew Jackson Downing, *Rural Essays,* ed. George William Curtis (New York: G. P. Putnam, 1853), xxviii.

4. Andrew Jackson Downing, *Victorian Cottage Residences* (New York: Dover, 1981; a republication of the 5th ed., John Wiley and Son, 1873; first published in 1842 under the title *Cottage Residences*), ix.

5. Delores Hayden, *Redesigning the American Dream* (New York: Norton, 2002), 34.

6. Alexis de Tocqueville, *Democracy in America* (New York: Harper and Row, 1969), 506.

7. At the 1931 National Conference on Housing and Homeownership, Herbert Hoover enthusiastically proclaimed, "To own one's own home is a physical expression of individualism." Brian McCabe, *No Place Like Home: Wealth, Community and the Politics of Homeownership* (Oxford: Oxford University Press, 2016), 42.

8. de Tocqueville, *Democracy in America*, 510.

9. de Tocqueville, *Democracy in America*, 511.

Chapter 4

Where Does the Christian Come Down?

THERE IS A DEEP and perennial human tendency to blame evil on one part of creation and seek salvation in another. This piece of bad theology informed a good deal of Victorian cultural understanding. There the city is represented as inherently bad (the source of sin and degradation); the family as inherently good (the source of spiritual regeneration and moral uplift). Consider a couple of telling lines from William Cowper, a poet popular with the Victorians: "Domestic happiness, thou only bliss / Of Paradise that hast survived the Fall!"[1] Did the family really escape the effects of the fall? Divorce and domestic abuse statistics speak against this piece of domestic romanticism. Wilberforce himself wrote of the high priestly function women serve as the "medium of our intercourse with that heavenly world,"[2] a vocation previously reserved for the person of Jesus Christ. Consider again Downing's claim that the suburban home breathes forth a spirit that purifies the heart and binds us to our fellows. In orthodox Christian theology, that is the sanctifying work of the Holy Spirit, not a house.

What is needed here is a good dose of the Calvinistic doctrine of "total depravity," if not for its own merit, at least as an antidote. The fall into sin has deeply affected all parts of creation—nature and culture, men and women, souls and bodies, reason and emotions, government and business, cities and families. It is not that one part fell and now threatens the unfallen part; not that one part remains pure and now provides redemptive leverage over the impure part. Both families and cities have been deeply bent out of shape. And both are candidates for redemption and renewal. There is no need to play them off against each other. Families can be a source of joy and a source of pain—and we should not ignore the pain. Likewise, cities can be a source of joy and a source of pain—and we should not ignore the joy. Christ-followers are called to work for the substantial healing of brokenness in both domains.

Moreover, good families and good cities need each other. Families are the site of human growth and development, and thus the source of presentable citizens. Cities provide the economic and cultural contexts in which families can flourish. Cities, however, as Greek philosopher Aristotle reminds us, establish the final context for the flourishing of human life across the board. Only in the city can the full range of human potential be realized. And it would seem that one of the dominant biblical images we are given to envision the future points us in the same direction: redemption takes us not back to the family in the garden of Eden, but forward to the city of God, the new Jerusalem, the divine metropolis enjoyed forever by the society of embodied saints. At the conclusion of the biblical narrative, in the Revelation to John, chapters 21 and 22, the visionary speaks not of souls being taken up into heaven, but of God coming down to dwell among us within the city of a renewed creation, where every tear shall be wiped away and death shall be no more, where flows a central river feeding the tree of life whose leaves are for the healing of nations. That bright urban vision, remarks Old Testament scholar T. Desmond Alexander, "represents the fulfillment of what God intended when he first created the earth."[3]

How should we work for substantial healing in our broken cities in anticipation of God's future? It is remarkable to me how little theological reflection has been devoted to this issue. There is a lot of advice in the Christian community about how to have good marriages and families. You will find a wall full of titles devoted to those topics at any Christian bookstore. Do we have any advice about how to have good cities? We have a Focus on the Family. Why not a Focus on the City? In the absence of much competition, here is my suggestion: work for good urban neighborhoods. Cities are made of neighborhoods. Neighborhoods are the basic units of placed-based human communities. Ideally—and traditionally—they are compact and walkable. They contain a variety of land uses and housing types. They are inclusive, not exclusive. For the past two centuries, Anglo-American Christians have been in the habit of taking one look at urban neighborhoods and moving rapidly in the opposite direction. Perhaps it's time for a second look—time to rediscover the virtues of urban neighborhoods, to recognize their unique features and assets, to appreciate their social and cultural diversity, even to consider dwelling in them and trying to make them both good and affordable places for others to live. Some of them are neglected and distressed.

But they continue to offer a viable built form for human community.

In what follows I am going to assume that those who identify with the household of Christian faith have a special reason for caring about the quality of our built environment. But should they? Should Christians care about the way cities are built? The proposition may seem strange. Questions about the design and physical disposition of buildings, the arrangement of land uses, streets, and transit may seem entirely unspiritual. They're about the material world, after all. But good Christian theology should convince us otherwise. At the center of the teachings of the church stands the conviction that persons-in-community constitutes the originating mystery of the world. That's what the doctrine of the Trinity is all about. One God, three persons—three persons in eternal, reciprocal, loving communion. In that communion, as Reformed theologian Cornelius Plantinga describes it, "each divine person harbors the others at the center of his being. In a constant movement of overture and acceptance, each person envelops and encircles the others," makes room for the others in an act of "divine hospitality."[4]

Early church theologians characterized the relationship between the three persons of the Trinity as one of *perichoresis*—quite literally, as one of dancing around together. In a free and generous act of creation, the triune God expands the circle of persons, calling human beings off the streets of non-existence into relations of love, joy, and mutual accommodation with God and with each other. The *Catechism of the Catholic Church* puts it this way: "God himself is an eternal exchange of love, Father, Son and Holy Spirit, and he has destined us to share in that exchange."[5] We are, in other words, invited to the dance. God is glorified—that is, the Trinitarian life of God is expressed, magnified, and made manifest—in positive forms of human community, where we too make room for other persons and help them flourish. What we find good and delightful in the human relations of friendship, marriage, family, in collegiality at work, in the fellowship of faith, in our neighborhoods, and in our cities has its basis in a reality that lies at the very heart of things.

Unlike pure spirit, however, human persons are embodied beings. We live in a material world defined by space and time. Our built physical environment will have a real effect on us and our ability to make contact with each other. The physical disposition of buildings, the arrangement of land uses, streets, and transit can serve to foster human community or to frustrate it; they can work to isolate others or incorporate them; they can reflect and inspire a sense of the common good or obscure it; they can pay attention to the needs and capacities of the human body or largely ignore them. By virtue of their theological convictions, then, Christians have one big additional reason to support the kind of urbanism that in fact fosters human community through the development of coherent neighborhoods. It's part of our divine destiny.

Notes

1. William Cowper, *The Task, A Poem in Six Books,* Book 3, "The Garden" (London: J. Johnson, 1785), lines 41 and 42.

2. William Wilberforce, *A Practical View of the Prevailing Religious System of Professed Christians, in the Higher and Middle Classes of this Country, Contrasted with Real Christianity,* 11th ed. (London: Cadell and Davies, 1815), 366-67 .

3. T. Desmond Alexander, *From Paradise to the Promised Land* (Grand Rapids: Baker Academic, 2012), 311.

4. Cornelius Plantinga, Jr., *Engaging God's World* (Grand Rapids: Eerdmans, 2002), 20-21.

5. *Catechism of the Catholic Church* (New York: Doubleday, 1995), 67.

Chapter 5

What Is a Neighborhood?

A PPLEBEE'S, a popular restaurant chain, invites customers to its doors with the slogan "Welcome to the neighborhood!" But Applebee's restaurants are typically located in parking lots next to car-clogged commercial thoroughfares on the edge of town. That's no neighborhood. A giant one-stop shopping store puts up a fake main street façade on its frontage, replete with false gables and non-functional windows. But it's no more than a big box with a 200,000-square foot floor area in a parking lot next to a car-clogged commercial thoroughfare on the edge of town. That's no main street. When it comes to neighborhoods and towns, we have much by way of nostalgia, but little understanding. We are cheered by the image. But we lack the reality.

The kind of neighborhoods evoked by Applebee's tag line— walkable, friendly, face-to-face human communities—do exist. They are usually found in the parts of our cities that were built prior to the Second World War, prior to the coronation of the car. They share a number of common features. We can name seven.[1] Post-war suburban neighborhoods have fewer of these features. None of them are to be found in our exurban regions.

Center and Edge

Walkable neighborhoods have an identifiable center and a distinct edge. You know when you're entering one; you know when you're in the middle of one; and you know when you're leaving one. Very often they have their own main street with shops, offices, plazas, squares, and signature restaurants. They support a strong sense of place while remaining open to the free flow of residents and visitors. They have gateways, but no gates.

Walkable Scale

Walkable neighborhoods are typically defined by a five- to ten-minute walking radius. That's about as far as a human body is willing to walk for something. Examine urban neighborhoods the world over—the Mission District in San Francisco, Park Slope in Brooklyn, Wicker Park in Chicago, Capital Hill in Seattle, Shadyside in Pittsburgh, Del Ray in Alexandria, Hampstead in London, Lindenthal in Cologne, the Marais in Paris, the Negen Straatjes in Amsterdam, or Banglampoo in Bangkok. They sweep out a quarter to a half-mile radius from their centers. Their size is dictated by a comfortable walking distance. They are fitted to the needs, capacities, and limitations of the human body, not the automobile.

Mixed Use

Walkable neighborhoods have a mix of land uses. In them you will find not only houses, but stores, offices, restaurants, pubs, coffee shops, schools, places of worship, post offices, libraries, parks, squares, and transit stops—all within a walkable range. Ideally, a neighborhood should be sufficient to meet a household's daily and weekly needs for provisions, recreation, and social life. You should not have to drive to get a gallon of milk.

Connected Streets

Walkable neighborhoods have a manageable block structure and a fine network of streets. They are easily and safely navigated by the pedestrian. The blocks are rarely more than 400 feet long. The streets are relatively narrow; the traffic relatively calm. The streets are lined by generous sidewalks. They are easy to cross, and they crisscross each other, making for multiple routes between points A and B. Rather than funneling auto traffic into one congested, pedestrian-hostile arterial, they absorb and disperse it. If traffic is backed up on one street, you can easily find an alternate route one or two blocks away.

Hierarchy of Buildings

Walkable neighborhoods are typically laid out so that special buildings occupy special sites. You can tell which buildings play important civic roles by their size, architecture, and location. There is a building hierarchy. Some buildings blend into the urban fabric. Others stand out. A common technique used to create a building hierarchy is the "terminated vista." Here a central street runs into a square or plaza where stands the special building—city hall, a library, an art museum, a cathedral. There it commands the view of all who use the street. It's given pride of place.

Public Transit

Walkable neighborhoods are connected to other neighborhoods and to the central business district of a city by way of public transit. Walking has its limits. Beyond those limits you should be able to make use of affordable, convenient, and reliable public transit—be it bus, subway, or light rail—to travel to other parts of the city. Driving is always an option. But it is not a necessity.

Mixed Housing Types
  Walkable neighborhoods have a variety of housing types and lot sizes. Within their bounds you should be able to find a detached single-family house, a townhouse, a condo, a duplex, or an apartment, depending on your financial means, size of household, and stage of life. In such neighborhoods it is not unusual to find a multi-unit apartment building anchoring the corner of a block filled in by single-family detached houses and duplexes. Or single-family detached houses with accessory dwelling units—"granny flats"—in the back. Or a row of townhouses across from a row of single-family detached homes. You should be able to live there if you are a college student, a young professional, an old professional, a service-sector worker, part of a young family, a big family, or an empty nester. When it comes time to downsize, you should not have to move out of the neighborhood if you don't want to. Genuine place-based communities are inclusive, not exclusive. The variety of housing types accommodates a mix of demographics and income levels.

  Seven features. None of them complicated or expensive. Put them together, and you have a neighborhood scaled and built for human beings in all their diversity. About 4,000 to 6,000 of them. Far from the one-size-fits-all approach of the typical suburban subdivision—where we are all to live in three-bedroom detached houses and drive cars—the walkable neighborhood offers a variety of housing and transit options. It expands the range of choice. It accommodates diverse human types, households, and preferences. One neighborhood by itself is a village. Put several neighborhoods together and you have a town. Add even more and you have a city. In some city neighborhoods a particular use will predominate. That makes of them a district—like an entertainment district or the central business district. In all, however, the neighborhood remains the basic building block of urban form.

Notes

1. The authors of *Suburban Nation* identify six components of traditional neighborhoods: the center, the five-minute walk, the street network, narrow and versatile streets, mixed-use, and special sites for special buildings. To this list they contrast the five components of sprawl: housing subdivisions, shopping malls, office parks, isolated civic institutions, and miles of roadways. I have modified the list of components for traditional neighborhoods, collapsing streets into one category and adding public transit and mixed housing types. Of course, such things as a building hierarchy and mixed housing types are not essential to a walkable neighborhood. But traditionally these elements have come together in one package. See Chapter One of Andres Duany, Elizabeth Plater-Zyberk, and Jeff Speck, *Suburban Nation: The Rise of Sprawl and the Decline of the American Dream*, 2nd. ed. (New York: North Point, 2010).

Chapter 6

Complete Streets

PICTURE A CITY. Chances are you have a street scene in mind. In her classic work on urbanism, *The Death and Life of Great American Cities*, Jane Jacobs captures this point: "Think of a city and what comes to mind? Its streets. If a city's streets look interesting, the city looks interesting; if they look dull, the city looks dull."[1] But streets not only form the outward appearance of the city. They also perform important functions intrinsic to the city. They are its "vital organs;" they "work harder than any other part of downtown."[2] Streets define the public face of a city. They also provide for both circulation and social interaction in shared civic space.

To gain some insight into the nature of streets it can be helpful to compare the city to a house. A house has rooms. Rooms are usually associated with certain kinds of activity: kitchens for food preparation; dining rooms for eating; bedrooms for sleeping; family rooms for informal social activity. The rooms are typically connected by hallways that make movement between the rooms possible. The hallways are defined by interior walls.

Streets are to the public space of the city what hallways are to the private space of the house. They are our shared corridors. They make movement between centers of activity possible. And they are defined by walls. But here the walls are formed by buildings. The exterior walls of the buildings that line the street serve as the interior walls of the public hallway. They give it definition; they provide a sense of enclosure. Ideally the buildings that line the streets at the core of a neighborhood are at least as high as the street is wide. Two or more stories high, they lend themselves to mixed use: retail below, office and residential above. If those building heights are less than one sixth of the width of the street, they will fail to define the street. The street is no longer a definite place. It's just an unprotected strip in the middle of space. To define the street consistently, the street wall formed by buildings also needs to be continuous. Buildings separated from each other by side parking lots will not do the job. Like a pleasant smile, the street wall should have no big gaps.

The same principle holds for public squares and plazas. These are the rooms in the shared civic space of the city. They are associated with certain kinds of activity: catching the sun on a lunch break, strolling with kids in the fresh air, sitting on a bench to finish a chapter of a book, listening to an outdoor concert, meeting friends and associates, playing chess, listening to a campaign speech, celebrating the New Year with others, ice-skating in winter, shopping at a weekly farmers' market, even attending a protest rally. And they are defined by the buildings that surround them.

Buildings define the space between them. That's why good urban design pays a lot of attention to the space between buildings, and to the relation between those spaces. Take, for example, the narrow space of a street and the open space of a plaza. The transition between them, from street to plaza, is known in the architectural world as "compression and release." It adds a sense of drama as one moves through the city.

Typically, the streets and squares at the core of a city or urban neighborhood will be surrounded by taller buildings. These buildings will be more formal in structure and placement. They will sit close to each other, making for a more compact urban environment. As you move from higher building densities at the center of a city to lower densities at the rural edge, the streets will become more open and at times curvilinear, the buildings lower and spaced out. Curbs will be replaced by swales, sidewalks with paths. Trees will begin to take over the job of defining space. Land use will become predominately residential. Those who thrive on street energy and want to live where the action is can locate in the center of a neighborhood or in the central business district of the city. Those who need more space, more privacy, more quiet, and more greenery have the option of living closer to the rural edge of town. Individuals occupy different points on the spectrum of needs for privacy, on the one hand, and conviviality on the other. A neighborhood, or at least a town, should be able to accommodate them all. But here again we are talking about manageable distances from center to edge. Within neighborhoods, distances remain walkable; between neighborhoods, they can be traversed by way of bike or public transit.

The study of the progression of the built environment from urban center to rural edge, and the typical differences in streets and the size and disposition of buildings along the way, has been captured recently in the theory of the transect. The idea of the transect was taken from the life sciences that study the progression of plants and animal habitats along a geographical cross-section. Take for example a cross-section that runs from the edge of a sizable lake, across the beach, and through sand dunes to a woodland forest. You will find that different kinds of plants and animals thrive at different stages of the progression. Rarely will you see a mature maple tree on the beach; nor will you discover zebra mussels on rocks in the middle of the forest. Likewise, in our built environment we should expect to see typically urban elements, like tall buildings and formal squares, in an urban context, and typically rural elements, like ranch homes and open roads lined by swales, in the rural context. In its application to the environments we build, the transect is an analytical and evaluative tool where the layers of the built environment, from the densest of urban cores to the open countryside, are distinguished into six transect zones with design guidelines developed for each.[3] Paying attention to the appropriate built form in each zone lends a coherence to our built environments and helps us prevent such errors as building a skyscraper in the countryside, running a highway through the middle of a city, or zoning for suburban-style retail in an urban neighborhood.

Streets and squares have distinct primary functions. One is to facilitate movement. The other is to accommodate activities. But they both have this in common: they create a public realm for social interaction. We can think of our social interactions with others on a continuum. At one end lie our encounters with complete strangers and at the other end our exchanges with intimate friends and family members. In the middle are our relations to what we might call civic acquaintances. They are not complete strangers. But neither are they intimate friends. These are neighbors you might meet on the sidewalks, in the squares, and at the local parks. They are the people you chat with about the weather, upcoming street repairs, the noisy party last night, the new restaurant in town, the last movie you saw, or the change in the local bus schedule. You wouldn't think of inviting them over for dinner. But neither do you ignore them. Social interaction in the middle of this continuum builds up public trust and social capital. It makes us less fearful of our neighbors, and it makes the neighborhood more resilient as regular communication coordinates responses to issues of common concern. What is sad about the disappearance of quality public space in exurban areas is that the middle section of our social continuum drops out. We compete, rage-ready, with total strangers for space on roads and parking lots in our four-wheeled metal capsules. We have close friends and family over for a pleasant meal in our private chambers. Gone are the many civic acquaintances made by face-to-face contact, often on foot, in the shared public realm.

While our public spaces have largely gone by the boards, we Americans invest relatively large amounts of our resources in upgrading the amenities of our private domains. What was once the public park is now our own backyard; the civic theater is now our home entertainment center; and the gym downtown has become our rec room in the basement. We hardly need get out anymore. Our homes are like all-inclusive resorts. Our shared public space—the visible representation of the common good, the physical stage of civic life, the place where we more naturally think of ourselves as citizens with common concerns rather than consumers with individual needs—gets only minimal attention. We are, as a rule, privately rich but publicly poor. That rule, of course, privileges the more fortunate among us. The rich have the means to create their own personal paradise; the poor do not.

The long-time mayor of Charleston, North Carolina, Joseph Riley Jr., exercised the influence of his office with the conviction that the development of quality public space in the city was important because all residents of the city, irrespective of financial means, should have access to places of beauty, delight, rest, and recreation. It's a matter of social equity as well as civic pride. In addition to revitalizing King Street (Charleston's main street) and overseeing the development of Charleston Place (a retail and hotel complex), Mayor Riley spearheaded the creation of Waterfront Park along Charleston's harbor. Nate Brown, a local construction worker, is one of many who have found respite in that park. "When I'm not working, I come here. Sometimes I just stay in the Waterfront Park and just relax and think."[4] The site of the park was first eyed by a developer who wanted to build high-rise office towers there. But Mayor Riley opposed the project, even though it would have added handsomely to the city's property tax rolls. "Great cities around the world," he maintained, "have to have the guts to give the finest parts of their city to the public realm."[5] At a recent national conference of the Congress for the New Urbanism in Detroit, he summed up his view this way: we know we've got our priorities right when "the things we value the most are the things we own together."[6]

A good part of the reason for the demise of the public realm has been the longstanding tendency to hand over the design of our streets to traffic engineers who seem to be convinced that the only purpose of a street is to move automobile traffic. The more the better. The faster the better. Streets were widened. Travel lanes were expanded. Pedestrians were pushed aside onto narrow and unprotected sidewalks. Bikes were unwelcome. Street trees discouraged. Public transit non-existent. Squares and plazas deemed irrelevant. Under the supervision of narrow-minded specialists, the street, the defining element of our public space, became little more than an automobile sewer. "Most of the noise, air pollution, danger, and perceived crowding in modern cities occurs because we have configured urban spaces to facilitate high-speed travel in private automobiles," points out Charles Montgomery in his book *Happy City*. "We have traded conviviality for the convenience of those who wish to experience streets as briefly as possible."[7]

The recent Complete Streets movement is a reaction against this sorry reduction of the street. Dedicated to the idea that public rights of way should accommodate all modes of transit, the Complete Streets movement advocates for street design that not only makes way for cars, but for pedestrians, bicyclists, and public transportation as well. Bring back the generous sidewalks protected from moving traffic by street trees, bollards, and parallel-parked cars. Pull down the elevated expressways that cut through our cities and divide our neighborhoods; convert them into grand boulevards that not only move lots of traffic but also enhance the properties that line them. Create bike lanes where appropriate by painting stripes down the street, or, better yet, install bike paths by separating bike ways from automobile traffic with curbs, medians, or planters. Run bus rapid transit on heavier routes with dedicated bus lanes, traffic signal priority, sidewalk ticket machines, and raised platforms for fast loading and off-loading of passengers. On the heaviest routes, lay down light rail that serves outlying districts. Make the streets lively corridors where pedestrians not only move but also pause for casual conversation or to dine outdoors. Let the streets once again support the social life of the city.

Notes

1. Jane Jacobs, *The Death and Life of Great American Cities* (New York: Random House, 1961; Vintage, 1992), 29.

2. Jane Jacobs, "Downtown is for People," *Fortune*, 57, no. 4 (April 1958): 134.

3. For more information on the transect, go to the Center for Applied Transect Studies, transect.org.

4. Debbie Elliott, "One of America's Longest-Serving Mayors Steps Down," *NPR Weekend Edition Saturday*, January 9, 2016, http://www.npr.org/2016/01/09/462400074/americas-longest-serving-mayor-steps-down.

5. Christopher Swope, "Public Officials of the Year: Joseph P. Riley, Jr., Mayor, Charleston, South Carolina," *Governing Magazine* (2003), http://www.governing.com/poy/Joseph-Riley.html.

6. Joseph Riley, Jr., in his remarks before the CNU 24, Detroit, June 8, 2016; attended by the author.

7. Charles Montgomery, *Happy City: Transforming Our Lives Through Urban Design* (New York: Farrar, Straus and, Giroux, 2013), 170.

Chapter 7

The Public Realm

WELL-DESIGNED STREETS and squares not only support social life. They support civic life. A viable public realm is where we meet and mix with others unlike ourselves. Yet in this realm we are given the shared space we need to identify, discuss, and debate issues of common concern. It's a setting for democracy at ground level. It's where we are to think of ourselves as citizens rather than consumers. It's an elementary school in civility. The lessons we learn there will follow us into our schools, workplaces, places of worship, and national political debates. For these purposes, the ungrounded, sometimes anonymous, and often vicious exchanges on the internet are but a poor substitute. In unfiltered public space, we don't get to construct our own information silos that simply reinforce what we already believe. And we don't get to attack others at a distance. We encounter others with different points of view and life experiences, which often prompt us to reflect on our own. And when we address each other face-to-face, as whole persons—bodily present, rather than reduced to avatars on a screen—it's harder to ignore the ethical obligation of mutual respect. We have an opportunity to learn how to live well with each other even with our many differences.

The mere existence of a viable public realm, of course, does not guarantee a good outcome. Some of the worst political movements of the twentieth century swept through the streets of the finest European cities. A sturdy moral order, a noble culture, a fair and functional economy, and a robust life of the spirit must also be in play. Nonetheless the public realm, as an enabling condition, remains an important factor in the mix. We ignore it at our own peril.

Consider the evidence. Sociologists have recently noted a connection between low density development and the quality of civic life. In his landmark study of the decline in American civic participation presented in his 2000 book *Bowling Alone,* Harvard sociologist Robert Putnam noted that every additional ten minutes in a daily commute was strongly correlated with a 10 percent reduction in civic engagement.[1] But he also noted a peculiar pattern of settlement in low density areas, sometimes referred to as "self-clustering." In the rush to the suburbs after the Second World War, "people fleeing the city sorted themselves into more and more finely distinguished 'life-style enclaves,' segregated by race, class, education, life stage, and so on. So-called white flight was only the most visible form of this movement toward metropolitan differentiation."[2] The loss of the public realm populated by a diverse citizenry gave way to areas filled in by the formation of separate like-minded communities, "little societies formed to our own taste," as de Tocqueville might put it.

Bill Bishop, in his 2008 book *The Big Sort*, noticed this phenomenon initially in the sharp increase of "landslide" counties across the states—counties (not gerrymandered districts) that went overwhelmingly Republican or Democratic. But when he scratched the surface, he found that the "big sort" was not just political, but cultural. In the exodus from the cities, people were moving and re-ordering their lives not just on the basis of economic realities and family ties, but according to values, tastes, and beliefs.[3] The result of this pattern of value segregation, in Bishop's view, is "balkanized communities whose inhabitants find other Americans to be culturally incomprehensible."[4]

The tendency to sort into culturally like-minded groups has not gone unnoticed by the real estate market. The developers of the Ladera Ranch subdivision for some 22,000 people in Orange County, California, had their antennae up and did their market research homework. They found that people fell into distinct value and belief groups, and built accordingly. In Ladera Ranch, each group can chose its own enclave. Composed of nine villages, the ranch includes "Covenant Hills" for those who identify as evangelical Christians, and "Terramor" for those deemed "cultural creatives." In Covenant Hills, the only gated village, the houses have large family rooms; the Terramor homes have instead a "culture room." Covenant Hills has its own Christian school; Terramor has a Montessori school. Although all residents of Ladera Ranch enter the development by way of the same drive, they soon turn off into their own cultural encampments.[5]

Bishop studied the sorting into like-minded communities of interest over a thirty-year period between 1975 and 2005. The result of the value migration was, more often than not, the construction of regional echo chambers.

Churches were filled with people who looked alike and, more important, thought alike. So were clubs, civic organizations, and volunteer groups. Social psychologists had studied like-minded groups and could predict how people living and worshipping in homogeneous groups would react: as people heard their beliefs reflected and amplified, they would become more extreme in their thinking. What had happened over three decades wasn't a simple increase in political partisanship, but a more fundamental kind of self-perpetuating, self-reinforcing social division. The like-minded neighborhood supported the like-minded church, and both confirmed the image and beliefs of the tribe that lived and worshipped there. Americans were busy creating social resonators, and the hum that filled the air was the reverberated and amplified sound of their own voices and beliefs.[6]

In the absence of a shared public realm, the civic conversation across race, class, beliefs, and values has been effectively disconnected. "Sequestered by income, deprived of parks, bankrupting Main Street for malls," notes Jane Holtz Kay in *Asphalt Nation*, "we no longer rub shoulders with our neighbors, rich and poor, deprived or thriving, that tousled mix of age, race, and experience."[7]

It is a natural human tendency to seek community and friendship among the like-minded. There's nothing inherently wrong with that. I do it myself. That's how we move forward with others in pursuit of the things we care about. We make common cause. The problem comes when those communities close themselves off and lose the experience, commitments, and skills necessary to meet the challenges of civic life. Studies to date indicate that this problem is more likely to happen in a built environment that sacrifices shared public spaces for private houses filled with people

who think and act alike. We lose the ability to relate to those
not like us. Urban sociologist David Brain puts it this way:
"The erosion of meaningful public space by suburban development patterns . . . is part of what has become a kind of
trained incapacity for public life."[8]

Life in the public realm, a realm that embraces genuine diversity, often involves conflicting interests. But that
realm need not remain a battleground on all fronts if we
are in a position to cultivate the skills and attitudes that
support and advance the common interests of civil society.
When political views conflict, Thad Williamson reminds us
in *Sprawl, Justice, and Citizenship*, it is important that the
parties involved "have a capacity to seek the common good
and revise their own demands in light of the reasonable
demands of others."[9] Private interest is often the reason we
get involved in politics in the first place. But under favorable
conditions and with some experience in encountering others
in real life with different perspectives than our own, that
self-regarding entry into public debate can lead to a wider
view and a consideration of the common good. Politics need
not always be a zero-sum game.

Civil discourse and debate at ground level is not confined
to public space in the strict sense, to streets and squares.
It also occurs in "third places." Neither home (first place),
nor work (second place), third places are where we hang
out. Described in detail by Ray Oldenburg in his book *The
Great Good Place*, third places are typically free or inexpensive, located on neutral ground, open to all irrespective
of social status, accessible by walking, visited by regulars,
and conducive to conversation.[10] They are the coffee shops,
diners, barber shops, beauty parlors, bookstores, lodges,

clubs, restaurants, and pubs that line the streets of a neighborhood. Privately owned but publically available, they too provide important places of social connection, serendipitous encounter, and ongoing discussion. As "settings of informal public life,"[11] they "represent fundamental mediating institutions between the individual and the larger society."[12] They are, in effect, the shared living rooms of the community; they expand our civic experience. "Without such places, the urban area fails to nourish the kinds of relationships and the diversity of human contact that are the essence of the city."[13] Moreover, they serve as local training grounds for civil discourse. A newcomer to a third place, Oldenburg notes, must be "capable of giving and taking in conversation, according to the modes of civility and mutual respect that hold sway among" the regulars.[14] At their best, third places have a civilizing effect.

Although third places are the natural manifestation of human sociability, they have been systematically zoned out of suburban housing subdivisions. This is unfortunate, in Oldenburg's view. In a subdivision with homes only,

> the individual's active friendships are greatly diminished, as is the ease with which he or she can make contact with friends. . . . Within developments that contain nothing but homes, residents are confronted with an unhappy choice: they may either open their homes to frequent and unbidden intrusions by friends or they may sharply curtail informal socializing. Usually, and with good reason, they opt for privacy.[15]

But a retreat to the private sphere which then serves as the primary site of reception for information about the world piped in via cable news or the internet has its drawbacks.

"An efficient home-delivery media system . . . tends to make shut-ins of otherwise healthy individuals; the more people receive news in isolation, the more they become susceptible to manipulation by those who control the media."[16] Better to process the news with others; better to test our opinions in a circle of diverse viewpoints; better to be checked and challenged before our prejudices begin to feed on themselves and lose contact with reality. For these and other reasons, Oldenburg considers third places to be "essential to the political processes of democracy."[17] Excluding them from residential neighborhoods may not have been such a good idea after all.

The quality of democratic politics in America has not only been compromised by the absence of third places, the loss of the public realm, and geographic self-clustering according to beliefs and values. It has also been damaged by class segregation brought about by exclusionary zoning—specifically, the exclusion of apartments from neighborhoods of single family homes; the separation of renters from home owners. Exclusionary zoning has its roots in the sad history of race relations in America. But over the years it has become even more a matter of class, partly as a result of federal tax policies designed to subsidize home ownership.

In 1910 the city of Baltimore adopted a zoning ordinance that prohibited black households from buying houses on white-majority blocks.[18] It was not long, however, before race zoning was overturned by the U.S. Supreme Court in 1917 (*Buchanan v. Warley*) when a similar ordinance in St. Louis was contested. In the court's opinion, the ordinance violated the freedom of contract. Home owners should be able to sell their houses to whomever they wished. After the court's decision, leaders in the city of St. Louis soon came up with another strategy that would pass legal muster but accomplish the same goal: in 1919 it adopted an exclusionary zoning ordinance based on class. No apartment buildings were to be built in neighborhoods made up of single-family detached houses. This would serve to keep lower class families (who were predominantly black) from living in middle class neighborhoods (which were predominantly white). Although the new ordinance made no mention of race, its intent was clear. Harland Bartholomew, planning director for St. Louis at the time, let the cat out of the bag when he said that the goal of the ordinance was to prevent "colored people" from moving into "finer residential districts."[19]

Exclusionary zoning received a significant boost from the federal government's desire to encourage home ownership. Prior to the Great Depression, when home ownership was promoted in order to stimulate the economy, the federal government was convinced that home ownership would make for better citizens. When the Industrial Revolution hit the states in mid-nineteenth century, millions of Americans moved from the country to the city. In doing so, they moved from owning homes they built for themselves on the farmstead to renting apartments in urban tenements. They were joining the swelling ranks of industrial workers. America was no longer an agrarian society of independent property owners as envisioned by Thomas Jefferson.

Growing tensions between industrial workers and industrial owners led to social instability and the threat of radical politics. Following the Russian Revolution of 1917, anxious government leaders at the federal level sought to discourage a similar communist takeover by promoting home ownership.

The thought was that homeowners would be less enchanted by the communist proposal to abolish private property. The Federal Department of Labor soon launched an "Own Your Own Home" campaign, a full court press of public relations efforts replete with buttons, pamphlets, posters, and newspaper ads. The National Association of Real Estate Boards, founded in Chicago in 1908, stood to benefit from the campaign financially. In 1918, the *National Real Estate Journal* came out in support of the effort, capitalizing on the Red Scare: "Every assistance should be extended to enable our people to build or buy homes. Where there is a community of homeowners, no Bolshevists or anarchists can be found."[20] Somehow, home ownership in America became not only a privilege but also a patriotic duty.

The Own Your Own Home campaign did not have much effect on the actual rate of home ownership in America. The real shift in that direction had to await the construction of a financial bridge by the Roosevelt administration during the Great Depression of the 1930s. Through the agency of the Federal Housing Administration, created in 1934, the federal government sponsored low-interest, low-down payment home loans fully amortized over thirty years. That made homes affordable for a vast number of American households.

A second boost came in the 1980s, during the Reagan administration, in the form of substantial tax benefits. The sixteenth amendment to the U.S. Constitution, adopted in 1913, gave the federal government the right to levy an income tax. At first, interest on all consumer debt was excluded from federal taxation. Later, with the Tax Reform Act of 1986, various forms of consumer debt were no longer excluded, leaving only the home mortgage interest deduction. As a result of this shift in tax policy, together with the exclusion of capital gains tax from the sale of a home, the home became desirable not only as a residence but also as an important investment vehicle, a significant wealth-building tool.[21] Federal tax policy created a strong incentive to shift debt in the direction of home ownership and to use low-interest home equity loans, where the interest is also tax deductible, as a cheap source of cash. Suddenly the home became a giant credit card.[22]

While federal tax policy is of great benefit to homeowners, it is not without its own set of drawbacks. As a tax policy, it is regressive. That is, the richer the household, the bigger the house, the larger the mortgage, the greater the tax benefit. The home ownership subsidy also costs the federal government a huge amount in tax revenues. According to the federal Office of Management and Budget, in 2014 the federal government lost $100 billion in tax revenues due to this subsidy for home ownership. The exclusion of capital gains from the sale of homes in 2014 represented an additional loss of $45 billion in tax revenue.[23]

One additional problem with the tax policy is its effect on the quality of political participation on the part of homeowners. In his recent book, *No Place Like Home*, Brian McCabe argues that the tax policy encourages Americans to view "housing as a commodity, to be bought and sold for a profit," and that this view in turn encourages "homeowners to engage in their communities as a way to protect their property values."[24] In short, the federal tax policy leads directly to the politics of exclusion.

Consider a recent public controversy in Winnetka, Illinois, a wealthy community just north of Chicago. The median price of a house in Winnetka is $900,000. The median household income is just above $200,000. Up comes a proposal for the construction of affordable housing in Winnetka by establishing a municipal land trust. The housing would make available affordable rental units for households with annual incomes of $45,000; home ownership for households with incomes ranging between $75,000 to $105,000. That is, for middle class people. The measure would, among other things, enable those who work in the community—teachers, police, shop owners—to live in the community they serve. But it immediately triggered class fear of renters. Winnetka Homeowners Association strongly opposed the plan, raising the prospect of higher crime rates and lower property values. In its publication, one resident warned of "the friends and relatives of the tenants: the crack head that is the father of one of their six kids . . . the boyfriend who just got out of jail and needs a place to stay, or his cell mate that got out early and needs a place to stay . . . the cousin who's on house arrest for a sex crime—living on a common wall with your 5-year-old."[25] This demonization of people of lesser means is a classic case of NIMBY politics,[26] fueled not only by prejudice but also by an anxiety over the loss of property values. An entirely misplaced anxiety, in my view. I live a neighborhood of mixed residential types: single-family homes, duplexes, four-unit apartment buildings, and a forty-seven-unit apartment building just two blocks from my house. I have not noticed a diminution in my quality of life for all the economic diversity. If anything, it has made for a livelier, more vibrant, and more interesting neighborhood. Moreover, the property values in my part of town have risen faster in the last six years than any other part of town.

McCabe notes a certain irony in the federal tax policies that subsidize home ownership. The original premise of the policies was that homeowners make better citizens. The aim was to increase the level of virtuous civic participation. But the policies so amplified the value of a house as a vehicle of investment that it became difficult for homeowners to think of it as anything other than the primary source of their financial security. The result was indeed an increase in civic participation, but mainly to protect private property values against all perceived threats. It led to the self-interested politics of exclusion, which does not strengthen communities—it divides them.

Traditional, walkable neighborhoods contain a mix of housing types. They are inclusive rather than exclusive. They accommodate a variety of households at different income levels. This accommodation not only fulfills the mandate of hospitality. If it reduces class separation, social fear, and baseless stereotyping, it may also improve the quality of our democratic politics.

Notes

1. Robert D. Putnam, *Bowling Alone: The Collapse and Revival of American Community* (New York: Simon and Schuster, 2000), 213. By "civic engagement" Putnam has in mind such things as voting, joining a civic organization, attending public meetings, signing petitions, and the like.
2. Putnam, *Bowling Alone*, 209.
3. Bill Bishop, *The Big Sort: Why the Clustering of America is Tearing Us Apart* (New York: Houghton Mifflin, 2008), 12.

4. Bishop, *The Big Sort*, 14.

5. Bishop, *The Big Sort*, 212-13. To be fair, I should point out that the residents of Ladera Ranch have some shared facilities.

6. Bishop, *The Big Sort*, 6.

7. Jane Holtz Kay, *Asphalt Nation: How the Automobile Took Over America, and How We Can Take It Back* (Berkeley: University of California Press, 1997), 50.

8. David Brain, "From Good Neighborhoods to Sustainable Cities," *International Regional Science Review*, 28 (2005): 224.

9. Thad Williamson, *Sprawl, Justice, and Citizenship: The Civic Costs of the American Way of Life* (Oxford: Oxford University Press, 2010), 243.

10. See Ray Oldenburg, *The Great Good Place: Cafes, Coffee Shops, Community Centers, Beauty Parlors, General Stores, Bars, Hangouts, and How They Get You Through the Day*, 3rd ed. (New York: Marlowe and Company, 1999).

11. Oldenburg, *The Great Good Place*, 16.

12. Oldenburg, *The Great Good Place*, xxviii.

13. Oldenburg, *The Great Good Place*, xxviii.

14. Oldenburg, *The Great Good Place*, 35.

15. Oldenburg, *The Great Good Place*, 61.

16. Oldenburg, *The Great Good Place*, 70.

17. Oldenburg, *The Great Good Place*, 67.

18. Richard Rothstein, *The Color of Law: A Forgotten History of How our Government Segregated America* (New York: Liveright Publishing Corporation, 2017), 44.

19. Rothstein, *The Color of Law*, 48.

20. Brian McCabe, *No Place Like Home: Wealth, Community and the Politics of Homeownership* (Oxford: Oxford University Press, 2016), 39.

21. McCabe, *No Place Like Home*, 124.

22. McCabe, *No Place Like Home*, 125.

23. McCabe, *No Place Like Home*, 126.

24. McCabe, *No Place Like Home*, 124.

25. McCabe, *No Place Like Home*, 99.

26. "NIMBY" stands for "Not In My Back Yard."

Chapter 8

Functional Zoning

IMAGINE YOU'RE OUT for dinner with your friends. You order a large pizza. After fifteen minutes of eager anticipation, you are served bare pizza crust on a platter. In a bowl next to it is the mozzarella cheese; in another bowl the green peppers; in another bowl the diced tomatoes; in still another bowl, the mushrooms. You are rightly disappointed. Don't they understand what a pizza is? All the toppings are supposed to be mixed together on the crust. That's what makes a pizza so good: the mix.

Urban theorist Leon Krier once compared the city to a pizza. Just as you expect a pizza to have all the toppings in each slice, so you should expect to find all the basic elements that make for a good city in each of its neighborhoods. You should expect to enjoy a convenient, interesting, and lively mix of housing, office, retail, civic buildings, parks, and squares. Instead, in functional zoning it was decided that these elements were somehow incompatible and should therefore be physically separated from each other. Hence the housing subdivision in one place, the shopping mall in another place, and the office park in still another. The city

hall cast at random on the side of an arterial. The park way
out on the edge, on left-over land. How strange.

The idea that different land uses within a city should be
physically separated came from the modernist movement
of the early twentieth century. Modernism, generally speaking, was the attempt to do away with the old and, starting
from scratch, reconstruct society along strictly rational lines.
Modernist architects, as a rule, had no use for traditional
cities. Those cities appeared too messy, too irrational, a
"picture of chaos," as one of them famously put it.[1] Not fit
for the modern age of the car and machine production, of
science and efficiency. Best to analytically separate out the
distinct functions of a city, siting each in its most advantageous location as determined by the relevant sciences, and
reconnect them all by the high-speed transit now afforded
by the automobile. Generally speaking, cities are built to
provide access—access to work, school, home, cultural amenities, goods, and services. The traditional city provides
access on the basis of proximity; the modern city was to
provide access through mobility. The "means of transport
are the basis of all modern activity," according to a modernist
manifesto of 1922. And those cities that do not adapt to the
means of transport afforded by the motor-car "will be stifled
and will perish."[2]

In the summer of 1933, a prominent group of modernist
architects met on a boat sailing from Marseilles to Athens.
On board they discussed a number of principles for city planning that would later be codified in the Charter of Athens, a
new vision for cities of the future.[3] They distinguished just
four functions within the city: housing, work, recreation, and
traffic. Each function would have its own exclusive location,

assigned to it after a careful study of climate and topography. "Land will be measured and assigned to various activities," (Charter of Athens, section 85) thus "bringing order to urban territory" (section 81). Space for recreational activity and broad highways would be created by building vertically, sweeping all development up into high towers in a park. The planning of what they called the "Functional City" would be under the control of specialists and technicians invested with public authority. No longer would it be left to "vulgar private interest" (section 95). Private interest must be entirely subordinated to the collective interest. If this program is to work, we must of course have "an enlightened population that will understand, desire, and demand what the specialists have envisaged for it" (section 91). This sentiment is typical of the modernist program for the top-down, theory-driven reconstruction of society according to a singular logic of machine-like efficiency. It thrives on elite culture; it has little use for participatory democracy.

In a later work, *The Radiant City* (1935), the lead author of the Charter of Athens, Swiss architect Le Corbusier, envisioned his urban ideal: "The cities will be part of the country. I shall live 30 miles from my office in one direction, under a pine tree; my secretary will live 30 miles away from it too, in the other direction, under another pine tree. We shall both have our own car. We shall use up tires, wear out road surfaces and gears, consume oil and gasoline. All of which will necessitate a great deal of work . . . enough for all."[4] Corbusier's dream of full employment based on dispersed, auto-dependent development has become in large part a reality in North America—and the nightmare of later generations who find themselves bound to a car and stuck in traffic. Adults between the ages of twenty-four and fifty-four now spend on average over an hour a day in their cars.[5] If the earth could dream, Corbusier's ideal would be the earth's nightmare as well. Cars account for roughly one third of our greenhouse gas emissions, putting out twenty pounds of carbon dioxide per gallon of gas.[6]

We can readily see the widespread influence of functional zoning across post-war development in America. Practically all land uses are now separated. And the car is the only way to get around. On average, 87 percent of the trips we make are by car.[7] The idea of towers in a park took hold in the downtown areas of our cities that underwent urban renewal in the 1960s—another modernist intervention. Four years after the close of World War II, President Harry S. Truman signed the Housing Act of 1949. In this act, Congress set aside federal funds to support cities in the "clearance of slums and blighted areas" (section 2). And cities were given the power of eminent domain to get the job done. Local authorities were encouraged to identify blighted areas, condemn them, acquire them through eminent domain if necessary, and tear them down. They could then turn around and sell or lease those areas for private or public development. The act made one billion dollars available in loans and another five hundred million available in capital grants.

The focus of the 1949 act was on the creation of low-rent housing. In 1954, the act was amended to make federal money available for the redevelopment of civic centers as well. It was bolstered by a Supreme Court decision in that same year (*Berman v. Parker*) that allowed the government to take private land not only for public use but also for more broadly defined public purposes. In both cases, the new, federally supported development followed the planning ideas of the Functional City together with Le Corbusier's vision of towers in a park—and his vision of what had to be done to create those towers. It is my "settled opinion," Corbusier wrote in 1925, "that the centers of our great cities must be pulled down and rebuilt."[8] Wherever urban renewal went, the fine texture of the city was erased. Existing buildings were demolished to establish a clean slate. Many streets were eliminated to create superblocks. The redeveloped areas were typically restricted to a single use: residential or office. Towers went up in park-like settings for housing and on vast concrete plazas for civic centers.

Grand Rapids, Michigan, was one of the first cities to go in for the complete redevelopment of its downtown area using Title III money from the 1949 Housing Act as amended in 1954.[9] In 1959, Grand Rapids invited to town John Paul Jones, a planning consultant from the New York firm of Ebasco. He blew in with lots of energy and big ideas for the complete reconstruction of downtowns using federal funds to cover two thirds of the cost. In July of that year, he proposed more than a million square feet of government office space and 13,500 new parking ramp spaces. Retail and residential uses were no longer part of the picture. They were separated out. In August of 1960, the citizens of Grand Rapid were sold on the plan to revitalize the downtown. They approved a 1.75 mill property tax hike to the pay the city's share of the redevelopment costs. In September of that year, Jones was appointed the new planning director of Grand Rapids, and soon the wrecking balls and bulldozers went to work, taking down all the buildings in a forty-acre, twenty-two-block area. The Richardsonian Romanesque city hall and

Kent County buildings were reduced to rubble. Sleek office towers were built on huge superblocks, creating a sterile urban environment that few would visit unless they worked for a bank, were called for jury duty, or wanted to contest a utility bill. The promised revitalization of the downtown did not happen. After 6 pm, the place is a ghost town.

The towers in a park idea was also used in the creation of federally sponsored public housing, known as "the projects." Between 1949 and 1973, the heyday of urban renewal, over 2,000 urban communities were plowed under and 4,000,000 individuals displaced. Most of the communities affected were African-American, leading novelist James Baldwin to claim that "urban renewal" was actually about "negro removal."[10] Many claimed with good reason that the new public housing towers were an attempt to isolate, concentrate, and contain the urban African-American population, keeping it from spreading to white neighborhoods. For the most part the projects only created dead urban spaces and social disasters. On July 15, 1972, at 3:32 in the afternoon, someone pushed a button, and the Pruitt-Igoe public housing towers in St. Louis were demolished. Built in early 1950s in keeping with the ideas of the Functional City, they were, in the end, judged to be completely dysfunctional. Some take that event as the official death of modernism in the realm of architecture. Not long after, Congress passed the Housing and Community Development Act of 1974, which focused on the redevelopment of existing neighborhoods rather than their demolition. Since then other public housing towers have been taken down, most notably Cabrini-Green and the Robert Taylor Homes in Chicago. They were replaced by, of all things, traditional urbanism—mid-rise mixed-use buildings on re-established street networks with a combination of market rate and affordable housing.

Perhaps a lesson should be drawn from the modernist experiments of the mid-twentieth century. Traditional urbanism represents the cumulative wisdom of building the human habitat over some 6,000 years of experience. It developed slowly over time by incremental acts of innovation and much trial and error as it adjusted to standing human needs and physical constants as well as technical advances and differences in local climate, custom, and materials. Modernism was a revolutionary program, born of a theory sprung from a few heads. But reality is wondrously complex and notoriously difficult to capture in a theory. Theories are inevitably abstract and often one-sided. Applying them on a large scale regularly leads to all sorts of unintended consequences.

Catherine Bauer, who was deeply involved in the formulation of federal housing policy in the 1930s and 40s, came to realize this point in retrospect. The modernist architects and planners, she wrote in 1955, "too frequently assume that there must be a *single* rational, logical solution . . . which results in vast housing projects that are apparently viewed by their designers mainly as huge pieces of technocratic sculpture, abstract forms that have little to do with satisfying, pleasing or delighting the occupants, as places to *live* in."[11] Later, in 1971, David Rockefeller, then CEO of Chase Manhattan Bank, rightly put his finger on the problem of abstraction, of focusing on one element of the urban ecology in isolation from others. The federal urban renewal program, he pointed out, "concentrated almost exclusively on housing and not on other related community activities. . . . The funds were not used to build a rounded community; they merely built houses."[12] Troubled urban neighborhoods were bulldozed; but what replaced them was only one element of the rounded community.

Tradition is certainly not infallible. And on some points—such as longstanding practices of slave labor or racial segregation— it is rightly opposed. But surely tradition deserves some respect, especially in areas of craft and practical endeavor. Why start with the idea that it needs to be entirely overthrown? What reason do we have to think that our big untested ideas will not just make things worse? Michael Pollan recently argued in his book *In Defense of Food* that our scientific/industrial approach to food has in fact diminished our diets and damaged our health. He suggests that we turn an appreciative eye to time-tested traditional diets, note the strong correlation between them and the health of their populations, and return to "real food"—unprocessed, without all the additives invented by people with chemistry degrees. Why not try something similar with respect to our built environment? Why not start with something like appreciative inquiry, where we identify, observe, and learn from what actually works, figure out why it works, and then critically and creatively appropriate it in our own times?

Notes

1. Le Corbusier, *The Radiant City* (New York: Orion, 1967; originally published in French, *La Ville Radieuse*, Paris: Vincent, Freal, and Cie, 1935), 189.

2. From a manifesto accompanying the "Diorama of a Contemporary City: Salon d'Automne," 1922, quoted in Le Corbusier, *The City of Tomorrow and Its Planning* (New York: Dover, 1987; a reprint of the English edition, New York: Payson and Clarke, 1929; originally published in French, *Urbanisme*, Paris: G. Cres & Cie, 1924), 84.

3. For one translation of the Charter of Athens, see modernistarchitecture.wordpress.com/2010/11/03/ciam's-"the-athens-charter"-1933/.

4. Le Corbusier, *The Radiant City*, quoted in Andres Duany, Elizabeth Plater-Zyberk, and Jeff Speck, *Suburban Nation: The Rise of Sprawl and the Decline of the American Dream*, 2nd ed. (New York: North Point, 2010), 3.

5. U. S. Department of Transportation, Bureau of Transportations Statistics, *Highlights of the 2001 National Household Travel Survey* (Washington, DC, 2003), 12.

6. Reid Ewing, Keith Bartholomew, Steve Winkelman, Jerry Walters, and Don Chen, *Growing Cooler: The Evidence on Urban Development and Climate Change* (Washington, DC: Urban Land Institute, 2007), 1. See: https://www.nrdc.org/sites/default/files/cit_07092401a.pdf. One gallon of gas puts out 8,887 grams of CO_2. That's 19.5 pounds. I'm rounding up to 20. The reader might wonder how one gallon of gas, which weighs a little over six pounds, can produce close to twenty pounds of CO_2. Here's how: cars burn octane, a hydrocarbon molecule composed of eight carbon atoms and eighteen hydrogen atoms. Upon combustion, the molecule is split up and expelled into the air. The hydrogen atoms combine with oxygen atoms in the air to form water molecules (H_2O), while the carbon atoms go on to combine with oxygen atoms to form carbon dioxide molecules (CO_2). The eight new CO_2 molecules together weigh a little more than three times as much as the original octane molecule. That's how we get 19.5 pounds of carbon dioxide out of six pounds of gas. According to the EPA, a typical car in the U. S., getting 21.6 miles per gallon and traveling 11,400 miles a year, will produce 4.7 metric tons of CO_2 a year. See U. S. Environmental Protection Agency, "Greenhouse Gas Emissions from a Typical Passenger Vehicle," May 2014, https://www.epa.gov/sites/production/files/2016-02/documents/420f14040a.pdf.

7. U. S. Department of Transportation, *Highlights*, 2.

8. Le Corbusier, *The City of Tomorrow*, 96.

9. For the details of the story of urban renewal in Grand Rapids, see the series of articles written for *The Grand Rapids Press* by Garret Ellison, published between May 18, 2014, and June 1, 2014. Start at: http://www.mlive.com/news/grand-rapids/index.ssf/2014/05/urban_renewal_main.html.

10. Quoted in Russ P. Lopez, "Public Health, the APHA, and Urban Renewal," *American Journal of Public Health* 99, no. 9 (September 2009): 1603-11. See also Jim Epstein and Nick Gillespie, "The Tragedy of Urban Renewal: The destruction and survival of a New York City neighborhood," Reason.com, September 28, 2011, http://reason.com/blog/2011/09/28/the-tragedy-of-urban-renewal-t. Originally, public housing projects built during the Great Depression and immediately after the Second World War were intended for white as well as black working class families. But they were strictly segregated by race. In the Pruitt-Igoe projects of St. Louis, for example, the Igoe towers were reserved for whites; the Pruitt towers for blacks. As white households became upwardly mobile and moved out, and the real estate industry successfully limited public housing to very low-income households after the 1950s, the projects became almost exclusively populated by blacks. See Richard Rothstein, *The Color of Law: A Forgotten History of How our Government Segregated America* (New York: Liverlight Publishing Corporation, 2017), pp. 32-37.

11. Catherine Bauer, "The Architect's Role in Urban Renewal," *Journal of Architectural Education*, 10 (Spring 1955): 37; quoted in Steven Conn, *Americans Against the City* (Oxford: Oxford University Press, 2014), 156.

12. Interview with David Rockefeller, *U.S. News and World Report*, June 7, 1971: 50-51. Quoted in Conn, *Americans Against the City*, 172.

Chapter 9

Jane and Goliath

T HE IDEA OF LEARNING from existing cities through close and appreciative observation is nothing new. The art was famously practiced by Jane Jacobs in the 1950s and 60s. And nowhere was Jacob's "ground-up" approach more powerfully illustrated than in the epic confrontation between her and city planner Robert Moses in New York City.[1]

An aspiring journalist, Jane Jacobs (nee Butzner) came to New York City in 1934 from Scranton, Pennsylvania. She moved in with her sister, then living in Brooklyn Heights. A couple months later, after a job interview, she decided to explore Lower Manhattan on her own. Emerging from the Christopher Street subway station on the west side of Greenwich Village, she instantly fell in love with the neighborhood's urban character. It was destined to be her home for some thirty-four years.

Jacobs began her career in journalism by writing articles for *Vogue* and other magazines. Editors were impressed by her extraordinary powers of observation and her ability to make ordinary aspects of New York City life into fascinating stories. In 1952, after a stint with *Amerika*, a journal published by the federal Office of War Information for the purpose of promoting American culture and values among the Russians—a kind of *Life* magazine for foreigners—she joined the staff of the *Architectural Forum*.

Two years later, Jacobs received an assignment to write a piece on an urban renewal project slated for the city of Philadelphia. She was given a tour of the target neighborhood by project manager Edmund Bacon. The experience was sobering. "First he took me to a street where loads of people were hanging around on the street, on the stoops, having a good time of it, and he said, well, this is the next street we are going to get rid of."[2] The very things Jacobs had come to value about the urbanism of traditional city neighborhoods were judged by city planners to be good reasons to tear those neighborhoods down. The next year, the Episcopal minister William Kirk gave Jacobs a tour of East Harlem, which had already been touched by urban renewal. Kirk felt like his community was under assault. Lenox Terrace had gone up, replacing three entire city blocks in his parish with eight twenty-story housing towers. Le Corbusier's plan was beginning to touch down in America with Title I money from the federal 1949 Housing Act and an army of ideologically driven modernist architects. Mammoth residential towers in a park were replacing the fine-grained street networks and blocks of existing mixed-use urban communities.

In April of 1956, Douglas Haskell, the editor of *Architectural Forum*, was scheduled to deliver a speech at a conference on urban design at Harvard's Graduate School of Design. He took ill just prior to the event, however, and asked Jacobs to fill in for him. She obliged. At Harvard the conference room was filled with academics and modernist architects fully on board with the wave of urban renewal projects sweeping across the nation. But Jacobs was not to be intimidated. Planners, she said, must "respect—in the deepest sense—strips of chaos that have a weird wisdom of their own not yet encompassed in our concept of urban order."[3] William H. Whyte Jr., the editor of *Fortune* magazine, got wind of her controversial talk and encouraged her to publish it. She responded with an extended article entitled "Downtown is for People," which appeared in the pages of *Fortune* magazine in 1958.[4]

Jacobs was unsparing in her criticism of the principles of modernist city planning, especially as they came to expression in urban renewal projects. "These projects will not revitalize downtown; they will deaden it."[5] "They will be stable and symmetrical and orderly. They will be clean, impressive, and monumental. They will have all the attributes of a well-kept, dignified cemetery."[6] The fundamental mistake, she claimed, lies in the planner's blind commitment to functional zoning, the separation of uses: "commerce, medicine, culture, government—whatever the activity, they take a part of the city's life, abstract it from the hustle and bustle of downtown, and set it, like a self-sufficient island, in majestic isolation."[7] Urban renewal projects assume "that it is desirable to single out activities and redistribute them in an orderly fashion—a civic center here, a cultural center there. But this notion of order is irreconcilably opposed to the way in which a downtown actually works."[8] Our cities, she feared, were being renovated by people who do not understand them.

Jacobs was not only critical of modernist city plans but also of their methods. Modernist planners and architects deal with scale models and maps; they look down on them from on high, assuming a hypothetical viewpoint some 30,000 feet above the ground. "We are all now learning," wrote Corbusier, "how to look at cities from above."[9] Like disembodied souls, they hover above the city. They do not consider the city as it is actually experienced and inhabited by human beings at ground level. For that perspective, Jacobs writes, "You've got to get out and walk."[10] The alternative method she proposed consisted of "simple old-fashioned observation," in order "to see how people actually use a downtown today; then to look for its strengths and to exploit and reinforce them."[11] She focused on streets and the features that make them both functional and attractive: visual detail, pedestrian furnishings, periodic points of interest, a sense of enclosure, a mix of uses—precisely the things the modernist movement in urban design wanted to wipe out in favor of the vast, clean, geometric expanses of the superblock. "The remarkable intricacy of liveliness of downtown can never be created by the abstract logic of a few men," Jacobs concluded. "Downtown has the capability of providing something for everybody only because it has been created by everybody."[12]

The *Fortune* magazine article led to a book contract, funded by a three-year grant from the Rockefeller Foundation. Jacobs began writing *The Death and Life of Great American Cities*, which she submitted for publication at Random House in 1961. The book has since achieved the status of a classic. In its pages she famously expands her critique of city planning. And she draws upon her own neighborhood, the west side of Greenwich Village, as a positive example of everyday urbanism: the narrow streets, the mix of uses in the buildings that line them, the generous sidewalks providing a stage for the spontaneous organization of social life, for private initiatives, for serendipitous encounters, for the daily the ebb and flow of sanitation workers, shopkeepers, school children, longshoremen, and families—all participating in a kind of improvised choreography in the public realm, a diurnal ballet.

Enter Robert Moses. Moses was a New York City planner of great ambition. The fine-grained texture of the walkable city irritated him. It took too long to drive through it. He wanted to make New York City safe for cars. Mayor La Guardia had put Moses in charge of the 1939 New York World's Fair. Moses used that position to promote his vision of the future. He invited General Motors to set up its *Futurama* exhibit designed to sell the nation on the idea of a country crossed by massive freeways, freeways that not only connected cities but ran right through them. He created his own fiefdom as director of the independent Triborough Bridge and Tunnel Authority, replete with its own office building and source of funding. He built the Cross Bronx Expressway at the top of Manhattan. Later he turned his hand to the creation of affordable housing. He cleared sixty acres in the Lower East Side of Manhattan and, in cooperation with Metropolitan Life Insurance Company, built Stuyvesant Town, a project consisting of thirty-five residential towers. The separation of uses, towers in a park, transit by private automobiles on limited access highways—it was the familiar modernist formula for the renovation of existing cities. And Moses had accumulated the power he needed to make it happen in other places in New York City as well.

At least he thought he had the power to make it happen. There was only one obstacle in his way: the citizens of New

York City. The site of his first big battle was Washington Square Park. Situated at the southern end of Fifth Avenue, in the center of Greenwich Village, Washington Square Park contains the iconic arch designed by McKim, Mead, and White that was built in the late nineteenth century to commemorate the presidency of George Washington. As chair of the mayor's committee on slum clearance, Moses proposed to take down ten city blocks of Greenwich Village, put in wider streets—the better to accommodate cars—and run Fifth Avenue right through Washington Square Park. The avenue would not only serve his new housing development south of the square but also connect to another project Moses long had in mind: the Lower Manhattan Expressway. As he envisioned it, the expressway would link New Jersey to Long Island by running straight through Soho, Little Italy, Chinatown, and the Lower East Side.

The plans for the extension of Fifth Avenue were announced in 1952. Alarmed, the neighbors who knew, loved, and used the park formed the Washington Square Park Committee under the leadership of Shirley Hayes to demand that the park be closed to all vehicular traffic. The city promptly set the plans aside. Undaunted, Moses came back in 1955 with modified plans for a submerged roadway with a pedestrian overpass. The neighborhood committee reformed in 1958 under the name The Joint Emergency Committee to Close Washington Square to Traffic. Now led by Raymond Rubinow and Jane Jacobs, the committee found high-powered support in the persons of Eleanor Roosevelt, Margaret Mead, William H. Whyte Jr., Lewis Mumford, and eventually Carmine De Sapio, New York's secretary of state. In November of 1958, the city decided to place a temporary moratorium on the proposed roadway. A celebration was held in the square with a ribbon-tying ceremony instead of a ribbon-cutting ceremony. In 1963, the plans for the roadway were permanently taken off the table. Moses was defeated.

Three years after the initial victory at Washington Square Park, Jacobs opened the pages of the February 21, 1961 edition of the *New York Times* to learn that her own neighborhood had been targeted for urban renewal. She suspected it was an act of revenge. Fourteen blocks of the West Village were to be marked as blighted, slated for demolition, and designated as a future site for the construction of residential towers. The area included Jacobs' house at 555 Hudson Street. Moses, it seemed, was at work again. The neighborhood she loved and used as a model of good urbanism in the book she had just finished was judged from on high to be a slum worthy only of destruction. Immediately another committee was formed, the Committee to Save the West Village.

Although Moses was successful, it appeared, in getting the West Village on the urban renewal agenda, he had already been relieved of his post as chair of the slum clearance committee. He had become known for his secretive planning and strong-arm tactics. In previous highway and urban renewal projects under his supervision, ninety-day eviction notices were handed out to thousands of families who were given little help in relocation. Tales of human suffering and displacement reached the papers. Moses had, in addition, displayed a real contempt for citizen participation. Obligatory neighborhood hearings were hastily arranged and announced at the last minute in hopes that no one would show up. His reputation tarnished, Moses had become a political liability. In 1958, Mayor Robert Wagner revised the rules for the urban renewal process in an attempt to make it more transparent. Responsibility for slum clearance in New York City was handed over to James Felt, then chair of the city planning commission.

But it looked like the Moses strategy was still in play when it came to the West Village: hatch the plans behind closed doors, then rush to implementation before the citizens had time to respond. Jacobs sued the city for not following its own policy. That bought enough time for the Villagers, as they were called, to prove to the city—and more importantly to the press—that their neighborhood was not a slum. The outcome of the contest was uncertain until Felt encountered another public relations problem. The planning commission was accused of making a secret deal with a builder, David Rose Associates. If true, the city would have been exposed for using the power of eminent domain to enrich the bank account of a private developer. A little sleuthing on Jacobs' part uncovered corroborating evidence. "First the builder picks the property," wrote Jacobs, "then he gets the Planning Commission to designate it [as a slum], then the people get bulldozed out of their homes. . . . It's the same old story."[13] The issue was brought up in a heated meeting with citizens at city hall. The crowd stormed the stage, demanding that Felt resign. In a panic, Felt called the police and left. The city got a black eye in the press and quickly backed off the project. The next year it withdrew the slum designation of the West Village.

But Moses was not done. Not by a long shot. In 1953, he had entered and won an essay contest sponsored by General Motors. The assigned topic for the essay: reasons why

America needed more highways. Moses had long dreamt of crisscrossing Manhattan with a series of highways that would connect the bridges and tunnels that spanned the Hudson and East Rivers. His vision got a big boost in 1956 when the United States Congress passed the federal Interstate Highways and Defense Act, which would provide 90 percent of the funding for interstate highway construction. Running an expressway across the borough of Manhattan, if it connected with the interstate highway system, would cost the city very little.

Moses was already building the Cross Bronx Expressway, which plowed through the Bronx against the objections of the residents and forced the relocation of 1,500 families. He then turned his attention to the other end of Manhattan. The Lower Manhattan Expressway, as he envisioned it, would extend from the Holland Tunnel on the west side of Manhattan to the Williamsburg and Manhattan bridges on the east. "Lomex," as it was called, would count as an extension of Interstate Highway 78 and thus be eligible for federal funding. It would run along the Broome Street corridor, widened 350 feet across to make room for an elevated ten-lane highway. That would require the demolition of 416 existing buildings and the displacement of 2,200 families.

Again, the citizens were alarmed and another committee formed: The Joint Committee to Stop the Lower Manhattan Expressway, led by Father Gerard La Mountain of the Church of the Most Holy Crucifix located on Broome Street; Louis De Salvo, the local state representative; and the indomitable Jane Jacobs. Even Bob Dylan got into the act with a Lomex protest song of his own. Again the city got bad press for its plans. It backed down in 1962. But Moses wouldn't let go.

He proposed a new version of the crosstown expressway, this time as a tunnel far underground. When that idea was judged too expensive, he then proposed to elevate the expressway eighty feet in the air. Jacobs resolutely opposed all versions of the expressway. Finally, in 1968, she attended a hastily arranged hearing on the project and led the citizens in a march across the stage at the front of the room. For that she was arrested and jailed for inciting a riot. But the press and New York City residents sided with her. Moses lost the public relations battle once again. Mayor John Lindsay declared the project officially dead on July 16, 1969. By then Jacobs had moved to Canada. Her husband, an architect, had received a job for the design of a hospital in Toronto. Besides, the Vietnam War was raging, and her sons were of draft age.

Notes

1. In this section I follow the excellent account of the confrontation between Jacobs and Moses in Anthony Flint, *Wrestling with Moses: How Jane Jacobs Took on New York's Master Builder and Transformed the American City* (New York: Random House, 2011), and episode number 200 of the Bowery Boys podcast, boweryboyshistory.com.
2. Flint, *Wrestling with Moses*, 19.
3. Flint, *Wrestling with Moses*, 25.
4. Jane Jacobs, "Downtown is for People," *Fortune*, 57, no. 4 (April, 1958): 133-40; 236-42.
5. Jacobs, "Downtown is for People," 134.
6. Jacobs, "Downtown is for People," 133.
7. Jacobs, "Downtown is for People," 134.
8. Jacobs, "Downtown is for People," 241.
9. Le Corbusier, *The Radiant City* (New York: Orion, 1967; originally published in French, *La Ville Radieuse*, Paris: Vincent, Freal, and Cie, 1935), 134.

10. Jacobs, "Downtown is for People," 134.
11. Jacobs, "Downtown is for People," 134.
12. Jacobs, "Downtown is for People," 242.
13. Quoted in Flint, *Wrestling with Moses*, 120

Chapter 10

Form-Based Codes

JANE JACOBS once said that she turned to the citizens of New York City because the planners would not listen to her. More precisely, they listened to her, nodded in agreement, smiled, and then pursued their revolutionary top-down approach anyway. Jacobs' ground-up approach, however, has recently found its way into the planning profession under the title "form-based codes." Developed in the 1980s by the urban design firm of Duany Plater-Zyberk & Company, form-based codes provide an alternative to modernist functional zoning. As the name suggests, form-based codes pay more attention to the form of buildings than to their use. And they are typically based on a careful examination and analysis of the best existing examples of urban form—those commonly judged by citizens and experts alike to be the most practical, enduring, and pleasing. Functional zoning will code an area for a tightly defined land use and then lay down some very general and abstract requirements for development: for example, the number of required on-site parking spaces given the floor area of a building; the required distance of the setback of the building from the street; or the maximum building height. The regulations are largely aimed at preventing bad things from happening, but rarely do they envision or promote the good. The design, quality, and character of the built form of the development, and the way it shapes and relates to the public realm, is left largely to chance. But overall, functional zoning as we know it makes for low densities, segregated land uses, automobile-dependent culture, and a thoroughly disappointing public realm.

Aiming at the formation of a spatially coherent built environment, form-based codes focus on precisely the issues left largely undefined by functional zoning. For a given urban context, they will specify the required height of the buildings (in the number of floors, not feet) in order to give shape to the space between them. It will mandate "build-to" lines to bring buildings up close to the street, the better to define it. It will require a certain amount of the property frontage to be covered by the building in order to form a continuous street wall. It will require a certain degree of transparency on the first floor of buildings in order to facilitate visual interest and communication between the interiors of the buildings and the public realm of the street. It will limit the width of buildings at the front and set maximum distances between their entrances in order to activate the street.

Although certain incompatible uses in a particular area will be proscribed by form-based codes, they are more open to a mix of uses, even in the same building, and to a mix of building types within the same area. In addition, they will carry specifications for what is often completely ignored in functional zoning codes: the streets. While functional zoning typically hands the design of streets over to traffic engineers, who seem to care only about the movement of cars, form-based codes will provide sections for various kinds of street types that mandate adequate room and protection for pedestrians, provisions for street trees and sidewalk furnishings, ratios between the width of streets and the height of buildings that line them, and specifications for bike lanes and public transit if appropriate. And form-based codes will do much of this—for buildings and for streets—by way of clear and precise drawings, making it easy for developers and the public to understand the requirements and envision the desired results.

Although it may seem that form-based codes are overly restrictive and would make for a boring uniformity in urban architecture, such is not the case. Form-based codes allow for much more freedom and flexibility in land use, which can change over time with the market and demographics. If retail, residential, and office are allowed on the same block, the proportions of those uses can shift as needed. And because the codes only specify the basic forms of buildings, the buildings themselves can be given different architectural treatments, from traditional to modernist to postmodernist, as long as they behave themselves according to the rules of good urbanism. Of course, special civic buildings, set out in special locations, can get wild and crazy. But they will stand out against a background of sturdy fabric buildings. The codes themselves need not be uniform across the nation but can vary by region and local preference. They are often the subject of a public design and approval process. In addition, they are usually internally differentiated with respect to transect zones, so that their requirements for buildings and streets shift as they move from urban core to rural edge. Form-based codes are where urban design and architecture meet, and there is no reason to think that good urbanism need be guaranteed at the expense of good architecture.

Chapter 11

The Many Modes of Transit

O N A RECENT TRIP to London, I took a non-stop flight from Detroit to Gatwick airport. After getting through customs and immigration, I took the Gatwick Express train to Victoria Station in downtown London, not far from Buckingham Palace. The Gatwick Express runs every fifteen minutes. Victoria Station is a big transit hub, offering regional trains to all points in southern England, a station for the London subway system, a bus stop, and a taxi stand. I chose the tube, as the natives refer to the subway system. Within minutes I was on the Victoria line to the Highbury/Islington station, no transfers required. Emerging from that station, it took me just eight minutes to walk to my destination. Just as it should be. A good public transit system should be able to get you within a five- to ten-minute walk of any point in town. And, of course, the point of entry to the system should be no further as well.

Cities and towns have many options for public transit: subways, light rail, and buses number among them. An intelligent mix of public transit, coordinated with neighborhoods and corridors dense enough to support it,[1] will reduce traffic congestion, minimize the need for the dead space of surface parking lots and parking ramps in the city, and make for cleaner air. It will also make for a more equitable and functional society. Roughly one third of the American population does not drive—too young, too old, too infirm, too poor. A viable public transit system makes jobs, education, goods, and services readily accessible to all. And we all benefit from that.

A growing number of cities have been exploring bicycles as a viable hybrid form of public transit, where bikes are provided by the city at little or no cost to the public for trips within town. There are no set fares or fixed routes. People bike where they will. But the bikes are owned and maintained by the city. Paris has its Velib municipal bike system; Toronto has Bixi; Washington DC has Capital Bikeshare; Portland has Biketown; Chicago has Divvy; and New York City has Citibike (which is privately managed). There are many advantages to using bikes for transit in town on trips too long for walking. They involve a moderate form of exercise. That's good for public health. They give off no carbon emissions. That's good for air quality and the climate. They rarely cause fatal traffic accidents. That's good for public safety. They are easy on streets. That's good for municipal budgets. And they take up relatively little space. That's good for cities, because less surface area has to be given over for parking. That's also good for water quality, because bikes require less hard surface than cars. Storm run-off from hard surfaces is a major source of water pollution. Bikes—both public and private—do, however, require special consideration on the streets. They are not cars. They are not as heavy as cars. They are not as fast as cars. They deserve a special infrastructure fitted to their needs.

In the summer of 2012, I was in Amsterdam and later in Copenhagen on a trip funded by the Calvin College Alumni Association to study the bike infrastructure in those fair cities. Both of them are known for their strong biking cultures—more than 50 percent of the commutes in their city centers are made on a set of pedals. Almost everyone, it seems, owns and uses bikes: moms and dads taking their kids to school in cargo bikes, students getting to university classes, professionals gliding to work with cell phones in hand, others going to and from the market with baskets brimming.

There are many reasons why we in North America have not gone for commuter biking in a big way. One big reason is that it doesn't look or feel safe. Most of our roads were designed for cars, not bikes and cars. This is where we might have something to learn from our northern European counterparts. They've devoted a good deal of thought and effort to making way for bikes in cities with the advanced design of an urban bicycle infrastructure.[2]

Amsterdam and Copenhagen not only have bike lanes, they have lots of bike paths. Bike lanes are created by painting a stripe down the street, marking that part of the roadway where bikes are given preference. But bicyclists are still exposed to moving car traffic on their left and often to opening car doors on their right. (In the bike community, the word "door" is a verb. You do not want to get doored.) Bike paths, by contrast, are separated from automobile traffic by a physical barrier of some sort—a curb, a median, or a series of planters. Bike paths are safer and, on average, increase ridership by 30 percent over bike lanes. The favored form of bike paths in both cities is an extension of the sidewalk.

Typically, the sidewalk takes up about eight to ten feet, then drops about three inches at a bevel, then extends five to eight feet for the bike path, then drops straight down six to eight inches to the street. After that, the roadway space is given over to parallel-parked cars or moving traffic.

Bikes are also given special treatment at intersections, where potential bike/car conflicts arise. Bikes going through an intersection will cross the path of right-turning cars; bike riders wanting to make a left turn will cross the path of through car traffic. In many cases, the cities of Amsterdam and Copenhagen handle these conflicts with special traffic signals for bikes. Bikes are given a green light while the right-turn red light is on for cars; bikes are given a green left-turn light while red lights stop through car traffic in all directions. In the absence of a special left-turn light, bicyclists will often execute what's become known as a "Copenhagen left"—a two-stage left turn where, keeping to the right, the bicyclist goes just over halfway through the intersection, pivots left, stops, and then waits for the green light. In Copenhagen, residents learn how to do this in elementary school. As in Holland, so in Denmark: all school children learn how to ride bikes properly in school. It's part of their civic education.

The urban bike infrastructure in these cities as we know it today has not always been there. Prior to and during World War II, bike ridership in the city of Amsterdam counted for over 80 percent of the commutes not by foot, the rest, for the most part, taken up by tram and rail. After the war, with a strong economic recovery and widespread car ownership, bike ridership dropped precipitously. Cars clogged the streets. Bike fatalities were on the rise. Eventually, in the 1970s, the Dutch bike community became militant, sponsoring city-wide protests and demanding dedicated space for bikes in public rights of way. In 1978, the government got the message and agreed to make the development of the bike infrastructure we see today a priority. Bike routes were planned, and, over the course of some thirty years as streets came up for reconstruction, the system was built, refined, and extended. Today Amsterdam, with a population of 800,000 people and 700,000 bicycles, has 400 kilometers (250 miles) of bikeways. Every day, on average, Amsterdamers log two million kilometers (1,242,742 miles) on their bikes. That's equivalent to 50,000 gallons of gas a day not burned.

The numbers are even more striking in Copenhagen. In the Danish capital, bikes outnumber people 560,000 to 519,000, and a full 85 percent of the commutes in the central city core are made on bikes. Today Copenhagen boasts 350 kilometers (217 miles) of bikeways, and there are plans for bike "superhighways" to bring more people into town from outlying regions.

The city of Copenhagen not only manages bike traffic well, it goes out of its way to encourage it. On a number of its major bike routes, the "Green Wave" (the timing of traffic lights to minimize stops) is set for the average speed of bikes rather than cars. When it snows, the bikes paths are plowed first, with only four exceptions (where bike paths and streets are plowed simultaneously). Although city officials are not averse to using the stick when it comes to the enforcement of traffic laws for bicyclists, they will often use the carrot instead. Recently city spotters went out on the streets of Copenhagen with bags of chocolates, rewarding bicyclists for obeying the rules at intersections even when it was tempting to break them. Copenhagen police went on a "Hugs and Helmets" campaign, giving free hugs and bike helmets to bicyclists as they stopped at intersections. (Bike helmets are not required in Copenhagen, but they are encouraged—in this case, quite creatively.) A great deal of thought and creativity has also been devoted to bike amenities: taxis with bike racks; two-story municipal bike parking racks; metal tracks on the stairways down to the subway stations to accommodate bike wheels; foot and hand rails to lean on at intersections while stopped for a red light; and, my favorite, dedicated trash cans along the bike paths, elevated and tilted to meet the right hands of bicyclists who have just finished their lattes on the way to work or school.

We might think the Danish investment in urban bike infrastructure must be the result of a different moral culture, a stronger environmental ethic, or the presence of higher ideals. That may be the case. But it probably isn't. The Danes are very good at tracking data. They recently conducted a survey of bike commuters, asking why those commuters chose to ride bikes rather than drive cars. Only 1 percent said they did so to make for a better world. The rest said they did so because biking was relatively cheap, fast, convenient, pleasant, and safe—all practical considerations. The city also conducted a detailed cost/benefit analysis of bike commuting for itself, taking all external costs into account (such as road attrition, surface parking area required, pollution, public health, and the like). The result: the city saves 3.14 DKK (about .53 USD) for every kilometer biked rather than driven. As it turns out, supporting bike commutes with good infrastructure is not only the right thing to do on many counts—it's also the smart thing to do.

Notes

1. A viable public transit system will need adequate residential densities within a quarter- to half-mile radius of its stops. (A quarter mile is a five-minute walk.) For this reason, transportation and land use planning must go hand-in-hand. Views on the level of density required to support public transit vary. But in general we can say that seven residential units per acre are required for a bus line; twenty residential units per acre for light rail (plus, by some estimates, twenty to fifty million square feet of office and retail in the central business district—the common destination of a commuter light rail line). Transit use increases faster than density between seven to twenty residential units per acre. This is because people who live in higher density neighborhoods are more likely to use public transit. Not only are there more people in the area, but each person is more likely to ride public transit. After twenty units per acre, the curve flattens out, because high density neighborhoods are more walkable—more people will simply walk to their destinations. See Jarret Walker, *Human Transit: How Clear Thinking About Public Transit Can Enrich Our Communities and Our Lives* (Washington, DC: Island Press, 2012), 109-134.

2. Information in this chapter on the bicycle infrastructure of Amsterdam and Copenhagen was gathered from the publications of the Fietersbond (Dutch Cyclists' Union), the Cyklistforbundet (Danish Cyclists' Federation), The Cycling Embassy of Denmark, and the Ministry of Foreign Affairs of Denmark, as well as interviews with Marjolein DeLange of the Dutch Cycling Embassy; Govert de With of the Dutch Cyclists' Union; Andreas Thor Hanson of the Cycling Program of the City of Copenhagen; Martin Akselsen, project manager, engineering department of the City of Copenhagen; and Camilla Richter-Frijs van Deurs of Gehl Architects, Copenhagen. See *Collection of Cycling Concepts 2012* (Copenhagen: Cycling Embassy of Denmark, 2012); *Good, Better, Best: the City of Copenhagen's Bicycle Strategy 2011-2025* (The City of Copenhagen Technical and Environmental Administration / Traffic Department, 2011); *Let's Reinvent the Wheel for a Change* (Copenhagen: Ministry of Foreign Affairs of Denmark, 2010); and *Cycling Cities* (Amsterdam: Dutch Cyclist Union, 2009). See also Ralph Buehler and John Pulcher, "Cycling to Sustainability in Amsterdam," *Sustain* 21 (Fall/Winter 2010): 36-41; and, John Pucher and Ralph Buehler, "Cycling for Everyone: Lessons from Europe." *Transportation Research Record: Journal of the Transportation Research Board* 2074 (2008): 58-65.

Chapter 12

Here's to Your Health

ZONING WAS FIRST invoked in the interests of public health. It separated heavy industry from residential areas. That makes good sense. Heavy industry is a point source of both air and water pollution. But now, some one hundred years later, zoning keeps practically everything apart—far apart. In doing so, it virtually mandates low density, auto-dependent development. We are now learning that this kind of zoning has itself become a threat to public health.

In 1996, the U. S. Surgeon General released a report entitled, "Physical Activity and Health." The findings of the report led to the conclusion that a sedentary lifestyle was a primary factor in over 200,000 premature deaths each year. It was second only to smoking in lifestyle choices that lead to chronic disease.[1] The Centers for Disease Control and Prevention (CDC) recommends thirty minutes of moderate physical activity at least five days a week. Evidently many Americans fall short of that recommendation. And it shows on the scales. A 2016 report of the CDC finds that 70.7 percent of American adults over the age of twenty are overweight. Worse still, 37.9 percent are clinically obese (where obesity is defined as a body mass index of thirty or above).[2]

The initial response of the medical community to expanding waistlines was to focus on the American calorie-rich diet. Dietary guidelines were issued. But they did little to stem the tide of fat. More recently it has taken into consideration the other half of the equation: the lack of physical activity. Even more recently, the medical community has become aware of the relation between the built environment, physical inactivity, and chronic health problems. In a landmark study in 2003, statistical research led by Reid Ewing of Rutgers University determined that people living in counties scoring high on the Sprawl Index "were likely to walk less, weigh more, and have a greater prevalence of hypertension than those living in compact counties."[3]

The Sprawl Index was created by taking into consideration four factors at the county level: residential density, land use mix, degree of centering, and street accessibility. These factors were combined to create an index ranging from 0 to 400. Lower scores indicate more sprawl; higher scores indicate higher densities. For the 448 counties studied, scores ranged from 63 to 352. The top of the index included such cities as New York, San Francisco, Boston, and Portland, Oregon. At the bottom were Atlanta, Georgia; Raleigh-Durham, North Carolina; and Riverside-San Bernardino, California. Comparing the extreme ends of the index, people living in sprawl areas weighed on average six pounds more than those in the most compact regions. The likelihood of being obese rises 10 percent for every 50-point move on the index in the direction of sprawl. High blood pressure follows suit: 6 percent more likely for every 50-point move in the direction of sprawl. The statistical results hold even after controlling for such factors as age, education, gender, race, and ethnicity. Oddly, people in high sprawl regions weigh more whether or not they claim to make a point of walking for exercise. Walking as a part of daily routine seems to be the key.[4]

The medical research thus far seems to corroborate what our intuitions might have already suggested: walkable neighborhoods are good for our health. They make physical activity part of everyday life. You don't have to take out an expensive gym membership or engage in heroic deeds of self-discipline in order to get the recommended levels of daily activity. You just have to live the regular life of a human biped and walk to the store.

But are the exurbs nonetheless healthier places to live because they are safer? Isn't it less likely that we will be killed by a car or stranger if we live in the exurbs? It would certainly seem so. Less traffic congestion would mean fewer traffic accidents. Less crime would reduce the chance of being murdered by a stranger. In 2002, William H. Lucy and Raphael Rabelais of the University of Virginia conducted a study of deaths due to traffic accidents and assault by strangers in eight major metropolitan regions of the United States. They examined traffic fatalities and homicides by strangers "to test the common belief that suburban territories, in a low density, quasi-rural setting, are safer places to live and raise children than cities and inner suburbs."[5] The results of the study convinced them that "leaving home to go to work and other activities is more dangerous for residents of outer suburban areas than for many central city residents and for nearly all inner suburban residents."[6] By "outer suburbs," the authors are referring to sparsely settled outer suburban counties, what we are calling exurban development. In the eight low density counties that skirt Minneapolis–St. Paul, for example, they found higher rates of death due to traffic fatalities and homicide by strangers than in the urban center. Between 1997 and 2000, there was an average of 237 traffic fatalities per year in the metro region of Minneapolis–St. Paul: 201 of those deaths occurred outside the urban center, and only 36 within. Most traffic fatalities occur on highways and two-lane roads in exurban and rural areas. That stands to reason: people drive at higher speeds in exurban and rural areas on roads with fewer traffic controls. In the cities, with lower speeds, traffic accidents less often result in fatalities. Empirical studies focusing exclusively on traffic fatalities bear this point out. "The higher the density, the finer the mix, and the more centered the development pattern," report Reid Ewing and Eric Dumbaugh in the *Journal of Planning Literature*, "the fewer highway fatalities occur on a per capita basis."[7] The researchers attribute this primarily to lower speeds in town.

But cities have more crime. What about the crime numbers? Doesn't crime make cities more dangerous than the outer suburbs? Granted, there is reason to fear crime. But given the constant media barrage of sensational crime reportage, perhaps we fear crime too much. Death by car clearly represents the greater danger. Traffic deaths outpace homicides in the U. S. roughly 2.5 to 1. In 2014, there were 32,675 traffics fatalities. In the same year, there were 13,716 homicides. In addition, most homicides are committed by people who know and are known by the victim. Unless you are a member of a gang or a highly dysfunctional family, your chances of being murdered, even in the city, are extremely low. In 2013, only 16 percent of homicides occurred in the commission of a felony, such as robbery.[8] In short, your chances of being killed by a car are much greater than your chances of being murdered by a stranger. The same holds for injuries. In 2013, an average of 6,336 Americans were injured in traffic accidents every day.[9] Injuries due to traffic accidents outpace injuries from aggravated assaults by more than 3 to 1.[10] And as we've seen in the Lucy and Rabelais study, your chances of being killed or injured by a car are much greater in the exurbs than the city. About seven times greater. Nevertheless, we tend to fear strangers more than cars, cities more than the exurbs.

It is a sad and ironic fact that many families move to the exurban edge of cities on the assumption that they are providing a safer environment for their children. But consider the data. According the CDC, the leading cause of death of teenagers aged thirteen to nineteen is motor vehicle traffic accidents. Between 1999 and 2006, 48 percent of teenage deaths were due to unintentional injuries, and 73 percent of those injuries were due to traffic accidents.[11] Over four out of ten teenagers get involved in a traffic accident serious enough to report to the police in their first year of driving.[12] Drivers between the ages of sixteen and nineteen are three times more likely to be involved in fatal traffic accidents than drivers twenty years of age and older.[13] Moreover, the risk of a teenager becoming a part of this sad statistic is greater in exurban areas. "The more sprawling the area the higher the all-mode traffic fatality rate," report Ewing and Dumbaugh. And the general data, they point out, are "confirmed for teens as well."[14] Teenagers in the United States drive on average

15.6 miles a day. But teenagers in sprawling areas are more than twice as likely to drive more than 20 miles a day—and at higher speeds—thus increasing their exposure to the leading cause of death for their age group.[15] "Tragically," notes Alan Thein Durning, "people often flee the crime-ridden cities for the perceived safety of the suburbs—only to increase the risks they expose themselves to."[16]

Compact, walkable neighborhoods come out ahead on the public health and safety scorecard. Eating real food is good for your health. But so is living in a real neighborhood.

Notes

1. Richard E. Killingsworth and Jean Lamming, "Could our development patterns be affecting our personal health?" *Development and Public Health*, Local Government Commission, July 13, 2013, lgc.org/development-public-health.

2. "Health, United States, 2016," National Center for Health Statistics (May 2017): 21, https://www.cdc.gov/nchs/data/hus/hus16.pdf#053; see also, JAMA 288 (2002): 1723-27. The rate of obesity for American adults between 1988 and 1994 was 22.9 percent; the 2016 numbers indicate a 15 percent rise in obesity rates since then.

3. Reid Ewing, Tom Schmid, Richard Killingsworth, Amy Zlot, and Stephen Raudenbush, "Relationship between Urban Sprawl and Physical Activity, Obesity, and Morbidity," *American Journal of Health Promotion*, 18, no. 1 (September/October 2003): 55.

4. Ewing, et al., "Relationship between Urban Sprawl," 52-55.

5. William Lucy and Raphael Rabelais, *Traffic Fatalities and Homicides by Strangers: Danger of Leaving Home in Cities, Inner Suburbs, and Outer Suburbs*, unpublished manuscript, University of Virginia, April, 2002: 2. See also William Lucy, "Mortality Risk Associated with Leaving Home: Recognizing the Relevance of the Built Environment," *American Journal of Public Health*, 93, no. 9 (September 2003): 1564-69.

6. Lucy and Rabelais, *Traffic Fatalities and Homicides*, 1.

7. Reid Ewing and Eric Dumbaugh, "The Built Environment and Traffic Safety: A Review of the Evidence," *Journal of Planning Literature*, 23, no. 4, (May, 2009): 352.

8. FBI Unified Crime Report, www.fbi.gov/about-us/cjis/ucr.

9. National Highway and Traffic Safety Administration, Fatality and Accident Research Database: www.nhtsa.gov/FARS.

10. Lucy, "Mortality Risk Associated with Leaving Home," 1568.

11. Arialdi M. Miniño, "Mortality Among Teenagers Aged 12-19 Years: United States, 1999-2006," National Center for Health Statistics Data Brief Number 37, May 2010, https://www.cdc.gov/nchs/products/databriefs/db37.htm.

12. Andres Duany, Elizabeth Plater-Zyberk and Jeff Speck, *Suburban Nation: The Rise of Sprawl and the Decline of the American Dream* (New York: North Point Press, 1st ed., 2000), 12 .

13. Centers for Disease Control and Prevention (CDC), Motor Vehicle Safety, "Teen Drivers: Get the Facts," October 16, 2016, www.cdc.gov/MotorVehicleSafety/Teen_Drivers/teendrivers_factsheet.html.

14. Ewing and Dumbaugh, "The Built Environment and Traffic Safety," 352.

15. M. J. Trowbridge and N. C. McDonald, "Urban Sprawl and Miles Driven Daily by Teenagers in the United States," *American Journal of Preventative Medicine*, 34, no. 3 (March, 2008): 202.

16. Alan Thein Durning, *The Car and the City* (Seattle: Northwest Environment Watch, 1996), 24.

Chapter 13

Balancing Budgets with Smart Growth

Imagine a residential block that is six hundred feet long. Now imagine two scenarios. In one, the block accommodates just six houses on large lots with one hundred feet of frontage. In the other, the block holds eighteen houses on smaller lots with thirty-three feet of frontage. The costs to the city for building and maintaining the block remain relatively fixed: it costs just so much to build the street and put in the water, sewer, and storm drainage lines; it costs just so much a year to maintain the street and the utilities, and to provide police, fire, and emergency services. One scenario is low density, the other approaches medium density. Which scenario makes more financial sense to the city? Which one is more economically sustainable?

City budgets, like most budgets, are built on two factors: expenditures and revenue. For municipal infrastructure, the expenditures break down into initial capital outlays for building stuff and ongoing costs for operating and maintaining stuff. Revenue comes from a variety of sources. But the single greatest source for American cities is property taxes, which represent on average 48 percent of the revenue stream.[1]

I will make up some numbers for the sake of comparison. Real numbers will follow. Let's say it costs $350 a foot to lay in the infrastructure for our block—the street plus the "wet utilities" of water, sewer, and storm drainage. That's a total cost of $210,000 for the six-hundred foot block—$35,000 per house on the low density scenario; $11,666 per house for the higher density scenario. Let's say the cost of operating and maintaining the block's infrastructure, and providing city services, is in total $12,000 a year. That's $2,000 per house in the low-density scenario or $666 per house in the higher density deal. In the first year, then, the city will have spent roughly three times as much per residential unit to provide infrastructure and services for the low-density development than for the higher density development. That's the expenditure side. On the revenue side, let's say the owners of the six houses in the low-density scenario pay $8,775 a year in property taxes, while the owners of the eighteen houses pay $3,500 at the same tax rate. The city takes in $52,650 a year from the low-density development, but $63,000 from the higher density.[2]

I don't think we have to pursue the math much further to realize that the higher density development makes more financial sense for the city. It involves less capital outlay and lower operating, maintenance, and service costs per residential unit; and it generates a larger tax revenue per area. If a city has to decide on the kind of new development it wants to sponsor, all other things being equal, clearly medium to high-density projects represent "smart growth" (which has become the name in some circles for compact forms of new development). After a detailed study of seventeen municipal budgets across the nation, the authors of *Building Better Budgets* concluded in 2013 that "Smart Growth is a much better financial deal for local governments and taxpayers."[3] And the real numbers back them up. They found that smart growth generally costs a city 38 percent less in up front infrastructure capital outlay (and thus less for ongoing operation and maintenance), and 10 percent less in the delivery of police, fire, and emergency services. More strikingly, smart growth generates up to ten times more tax revenue than low-density suburban development.[4]

The numbers are just as striking when we focus on retail instead of residential development. If we consider the city just from the business side of things, we can think of the land it incorporates as its raw material, the infrastructure and services it provides as the value it adds to the land, and property taxes as the return on its investment. The question before us: which style of development delivers a better return on the city's investment?

The difference in tax revenues between urban and exurban retail development comes into sharp relief when those revenues are compared on the basis of land area. Joe Minicozzi, from the planning firm Urban3 in Asheville, North Carolina, draws an instructive comparison from his home town.[5] The local Walmart takes up 34 acres of land on the outskirts of the municipality. The building itself covers 220,000 square feet. Its taxable value is $20,000,000. A considerable sum. A downtown six-story mixed-use building (retail below, office and residential above) stands on just two tenths of an acre. It comprises 54,000 square feet. It's taxable value is $11,000,000. Almost half the value of the Walmart.

Which one is more productive of tax revenue for the city of Asheville? If we look at just the raw dollar amount, the Walmart out-performs the downtown mixed-use building. But if we consider tax revenue per acre, we get a very different picture. The Walmart produces $6,500 in property taxes a year per acre. The downtown mixed-use building produces $634,000 in property taxes a year per acre. Almost 100 times as much. In addition, the Walmart generates 5.9 jobs per acre; the downtown building, 73.7 jobs per acre. From the financial standpoint, urban development is a much more efficient use of land than exurban development.

Some may wonder if the city's income from retail sales tax would change this picture significantly. Perhaps it would reverse our judgment. The Walmart enjoys a huge volume of retail sales. The city gets a portion of the sales tax. Sales tax, and the proportion cities get from sales tax, varies state by state, city by city. In Asheville, the sales tax is 8 percent, and the city gets 27 percent of that tax. Walmart produces $47,500 in sales tax revenue for the city each year per acre. The downtown building produces $83,600 in sales tax revenue for the city each year per acre. For the final calculation of the combined revenue from property and sales taxes, the property tax on each side needs to be limited to the part that goes directly to the city: $3,300 per year per acre from Walmart; $330,000 per year per acre from the downtown building. When the net property and sales tax income are added together in our example, it turns out that Walmart produces $50,800 per acre for the city each year. But the downtown building produces $413,600 per acre per year. Even when sales tax is included in the calculations, urban development far outstrips exurban development in return on investment.

When faced with budget crises, city officials often feel that they must either raise tax rates or cut services. But there is a third option: exploit the potential of property tax revenues through denser forms of development. Denser forms of development not only increase tax revenue yields, they also reduce infrastructure costs. They are more financially sustainable.

In their own analyses of infrastructure costs, cities, counties, and states have come to a similar conclusion. Consider their cost projections. The state of Maryland found that pursuing a smart growth program would save the state $1.5 billion per year statewide on new road construction through 2030.[6] This approach would reduce overall costs to the state by 28 percent and costs to municipalities by 60 percent. The state of California calculated that smart growth development would reduce infrastructure costs by $32 billion through 2050.[7] Smart growth also reduces the ongoing costs of city services. The city of Champaign, Illinois determined that smart growth would reduce city services costs by 23 percent over a span of twenty years. Fresno, California projected a 9 percent reduction in service costs; Nashville-Davidson County, Tennessee, a 13 percent reduction.[8]

The numbers on the revenue side also speak in favor of compact development. In a planning study called "Vision California," the state of California calculated that on a per-acre basis, smart growth would produce three and half times the revenue as low-density suburban development.[9] The city of Raleigh, North Carolina found that a six-story building downtown would generate fifty times as much property tax revenue as a Walmart store of comparable square footage on the edge of town. We can also think of these scenarios in terms of payback periods. Sarasota, Florida discovered that a compact residential project requiring $5.7 million in infrastructure generated $1.98 million each year in property taxes. That's a three-year payback. A comparable low-density residential project in the area required $10 million in infrastructure but only produced $239,000 a year in tax revenues—a forty-two-year payback. After twenty years, the compact project will have produced $33 million in tax revenue beyond the initial infrastructure outlay; the low-density development will still be in the hole.[10]

Those of us with some experience in household management know that balancing the budget is a lot easier when revenues outpace expenditures. And when things get tight, we often look for more efficiencies on the expenditure side and more return on investments on the revenue side. Cities face similar issues—acutely, in many cases, because of the reduction in property tax revenue in the wake of the four-year Great Recession that began in late 2007. There are many reasons to think that compact, walkable, mixed-use, transit-friendly neighborhoods are the right way to go. A look at municipal balance sheets might also convince us that they are the smart way to grow. It just makes good financial sense.

Notes

1. William Fulton, et al., *Building Better Budgets: A National Examination of the Fiscal Benefits of Smart Growth Development* (Washington, DC: Smart Growth America Report, May, 2013), 5. See https://smartgrowthamerica.org/resources/building-better-budgets-a-national-examination-of-the-fiscal-benefits-of-smart-growth-development/

2. Here I am assuming we are living in the reasonably priced real estate market of the Midwest. I put the market value of the large-lot homes at $500,000 and the market price of the medium-lot home at $200,000. Taxable value for each is roughly 50 percent of market value. Property tax is set around 3.5 percent. We could change the numbers if we like. But if we change them proportionally, we will get the same proportional results: the city will pay roughly three times as much for infrastructure per residential unit on the low-density scenario, and it will collect less in property tax by area.

3. Fulton et al., *Building Better Budgets*, 3.

4. Fulton et al., *Building Better Budgets*, ii-iii.

5. For information on the Asheville example, see: Joe Minicozzi, "The Smart Math of Mixed Use Development," *Planetizen*, January 23, 2012, https://www.planetizen.com/node/53922. Darren Dahl, "Why Downtown Development May be More Affordable than the Suburbs," *Forbes*, March 14, 2014, https://www.forbes.com/sites/citi/2014/03/14/why-downtown-development-may-be-more-affordable-than-the-suburbs/#137ff8a55bde. Emily Badger, "The Simple Math that Can Save Cities from Bankruptcy," *Atlantic Cities*, March 30, 2012, https://www.citylab.com/life/2012/03/simple-math-can-save-cities-bankruptcy/1629/. Joe Minicozzi, "Thinking Differently about Development," *Government Finance Review*, August, 2013: 44-48; http://www.gfoa.org/sites/default/files/GFR_AUG_13_44.pdf.

6. Fulton et al., *Building Better Budgets*, 4.

7. Fulton et al., *Building Better Budgets*, 4.

8. Fulton et al., *Building Better Budgets*, 5.

9. Fulton et al., *Building Better Budgets*, 6.

10. Fulton et al., *Building Better Budgets*, 8.

Chapter 14

Green Cities

W<small>E OFTEN THINK</small> of nature and the city in opposition to each other. Cities: paved and polluted. Natural areas: green and pristine. High-density development with its lack of green space seems like a threat to the natural environment. Maybe nature would be better off if we didn't have cities, the source of so much energy consumption and pollution. Perhaps the natural environment would be better served by low-density development, by the expansion of our leafy suburbs.

As it turns out, if we consider one of the chief threats to the natural environment—climate change—nothing could be further from the truth. The leafy suburbs are more likely the danger here, not the cities. Bryan Walsh, writing for *Time* magazine, wisely connected the dots between climate change and low-density development:

> Technology has gotten us into the climate change mess, and we assume that technology will get us out of it. Hybrid cars, wind turbines, algae biofuel—business and policymakers are searching for the technological fixes that will decarbonize our

lives. . . . The dominant pattern of development in America—large houses and sprawling, auto-dependent suburbs—requires a heavy input of fossil fuels and an output of carbon emissions. The adoption of cleaner technologies will take us part of the way, but what we really need to do is change our habitat, not just for the environmental benefits, but for our health, lifestyle and happiness.[1]

A study based on projections by the U. S. Department of Energy's Energy Information Administration bears this point out. Using 2005 as a baseline and 2030 as the endpoint, researchers predicted that at the current rate of low-density development, vehicle miles traveled (VMT) will rise by 60 percent. Say we increase the average gas mileage of our cars by 30 percent in the same period of time. Given these two numbers, CO_2 emissions will still go up by 12 percent.[2] To bring that number down, we will need not only high-tech solutions for higher gas mileage, but the low-tech resolve to build more walkable neighborhoods connected by public transit. Low-density development means more driving. More driving means more CO_2 in the atmosphere. More CO_2 in the atmosphere means more climate change. Between 1969 and 2009, the heyday of low-density development, the population of the United States increased by 44 percent. But the total number of vehicles went up 78 percent. During the same period of time, even though the number of persons per household shrank by 21 percent, the number of vehicle miles traveled per household went up 179 percent. The percentage of households that own three or more cars went from 5 percent in 1969 to 23 percent in 2009.[3] More cars per household; more miles per household. That's altogether bad news for nature.

Numbers like these convinced journalist David Owen that compact, walkable cities are in fact an environmental blessing. In his book *Green Metropolis*, he directs attention to one of our densest urban centers: New York City. If we focus on energy use by land area, New York doesn't look particularly good. In fact, it looks like an ecological disaster. Lots of energy is burned up within the five boroughs. But if we consider energy use *per capita*, we get a very different picture. The average number of metric tons of CO_2 emissions per person per year for U. S. residents is 24.5. The average number of metric tons of CO_2 emissions for the residents of New York City is 7.1. That's a 71 percent reduction. Residents of Vermont, a largely rural state, burn on average 545 gallons of gas a year. Compare that to 146 gallons a year for residents of New York. Those who live in the borough of Manhattan use on average only 90 gallons a year. Although New York City contains 2.7 percent of the U. S. population, it generates only 1 percent of its greenhouse gas emissions. That, if anything, is an environmental success story. And it happened not because New Yorkers care that much more about the environment. Or because the city is on the cutting edge of energy-saving technology. A big part of the explanation for this reduction is the fact that New Yorkers live in walkable neighborhoods served by public transportation. They drive less.[4]

We see similar numbers for new developments built in line with the principles of traditional urbanism. Take Atlantic Station for example. Built on 138 acres of old industrial land in the middle of Atlanta, Atlantic Station offers mixed-use development and a connected network of streets with convenient public transit options. It's compact and walkable.

It contains 5,000 residential units, six million square feet of office space, and two million square feet of retail, plus eleven acres of green space. At the time of development, the average number of vehicle miles traveled per person per day in Atlanta was 34. The goal of the developers was to bring that VMT number down to 25.5 for the residents of Atlantic Station. After the new neighborhood was built out and fully occupied, the 2008 data indicated that the residents of Atlantic Station put in just 14 VMT per person per day—a 59 percent reduction in driving compared to the city average.[5]

The general correlation between population density and VMT is striking. At one household per net acre, the average household will rack up some 30,000 VMT per year. At fifty households per net acre, the number drops dramatically, down to 7,500 VMT.[6] People who live in Seattle neighborhoods like Fern Hill, with densities of forty people or more per acre, drive two thirds less than those who live in low density areas with less than twelve people per acre.[7] Of course, there is much that could be done to reduce stormwater run-off in cities, to increase their tree canopies, to better insulate their buildings, and to encourage more comprehensive recycling programs. But on energy efficiency, compact cities come out way ahead on the environmental scorecard just by virtue of being compact.[8]

Notes

1. Bryan Walsh, "How Green is Your Neighborhood?" *Time*, December 19, 2007, http://content.time.com/time/health/article/0,8599,1696857,00. html.

2. See https://www.smartgrowthamerica.org/app/legacy/documents/exec2.pdf. See also U. S. Department of Transportation, Research and Innovative Technology Administration, "Transportation Vision for 2030: Ensuring personal freedom and economic vitality for a nation on the move," January 2008, https://www.rita.dot.gov/sites/default/files/rita_ archives/rita_publications/transportation_vision_2030/pdf/entire.pdf; Reid Ewing, Keith Bartholomew, Steve Winkelman, Jerry Walters, and Don Chen, *Growing Cooler: Evidence on Urban Development and Climate Change*, Washington, DC: Urban Land Institute, 2008.

3. See U. S. Department of Transportation, Federal Highway Administration, A. Santos, N. McGuckin, H.Y. Nakamoto, D. Gray, and S. Liss, "Summary of Travel Trends: 2009 National Household Travel Survey," http://nhts.ornl.gov/2009/pub/stt.pdf.

4. David Owen, *Green Metropolis* (New York: Riverhead, 2009), 2-3; 14; 17.

5. United States Environmental Protection Agency (EPA), "Atlantic Station (Atlantic Steel Site Rehabilitation Project)," n.d., https://www.epa.gov/smartgrowth/atlantic-station-atlantic-steel-site-redevelopment-project.

6. John Holtzclaw, Robert Clear, Hank Dittmar, David Goldstein, and Peter Haas, "Location Efficiency: Neighborhood and Socio-economic characteristics determine auto ownership and use studies in Chicago, Los Angeles and San Francisco," *Transportation Planning Technology* 25, no. 1 (2002): 1-27.

7. Alan Thein Durning, *The Car and the City* (Seattle: Northwest Environment Watch, 1996), 15.

8. It is tempting to think that reliance on the private automobile will not be an environmental problem once we switch over to electric vehicles. They don't burn gas, so no CO_2 emissions. But a lot depends on how the electricity that charges them is generated: if by coal, electric vehicles will actually make things worse. In addition, the production and discard of car batteries require energy and promise to increase the toxicity of the environment in their own ways (with lead, and sulfur and nitrogen oxides). See Troy R. Hawkins, Bhawna Singh, Guillaume Majeau-Bettez,

and Anders Hammer Strømman, "Comparative Environmental Life Cycle Assessment of Conventional and Electric Vehicles," *Journal of Industrial Ecology* 17, no.1 (2012): 53-64; and, David L. McCleese and Peter T. LaPuma, "Using Monte Carlo Simulation in Life Cycle Assessment for Electric and Internal Combustion Vehicles," *International Journal of Life Cycle Assessment* 7, no. 4 (2002): 230-236.

Chapter 15

The G Word

I MENTIONED EARLIER that exurban development is a recent and historically unprecedented pattern of human settlement. We are just now realizing many of its consequences. And many of its drawbacks: the transportation expense, the commuter stress, the social isolation, and, quite frankly, the boredom for lack of cultural amenities. For that reason and others there has been a renewed interest in walkable urban neighborhoods among middle- and high-income households. And there has been no shortage of mayors who are providing incentives for these households to move back into their cities in order to enhance the tax base. The shifting and growing demand for urban neighborhoods and their amenities leads to higher property values and an influx of higher income households into city sectors that are sometimes distressed and occupied by lower income households. And this trend sometimes leads to the involuntary displacement of lower income households due to rising rents and property taxes. The poor are priced out by the rich. This process is known as "gentrification."

Gentrification is a controversial issue. In 1999, a candidate for the office of mayor in the city of San Francisco pledged to declare "war on any and all gentrification."[1] More recently, a newly opened art gallery in the Boyle Heights neighborhood of Los Angeles was vandalized and its patrons attacked by local residents who feared it was the first sign of gentrification.[2] Indeed, it is often the object of wholesale condemnation. But gentrification is a complex phenomenon, more complex than many of its detractors or supporters will allow. It calls for a nuanced response. Economic change often brings unwelcome social and cultural change in its wake. And those changes are often, but not always, overlaid by issues of race and racism.[3] Yet re-investment and the revitalization of deeply distressed neighborhoods improve the quality of the neighborhood and city services for all who live there. In addition, rising property values build equity for all current homeowners. Surely opponents of gentrification across the board can't mean that we need bad neighborhoods for poor people. "I don't see anything romantic about poverty," reports Majora Carter, well-known resident and community activist in the South Bronx.[4] Re-investment in seriously broken neighborhoods is a good thing. But clearly involuntary displacement is a bad thing.

Part of what makes the gentrification issue complicated is the question of the base state of a neighborhood prior to gentrification. I am focusing my remarks on neighborhoods that have suffered severe disinvestment in the wake of post-war suburbanization, "seriously broken" neighborhoods—neighborhoods burdened by vacant lots, abandoned buildings, inadequate city services, lack of jobs, and troubled schools. In such cases, one can see some benefits in gentrification if it brings in its train genuine improvements. But in other cases, where the base state of the neighborhood is perfectly functional, if humble, it is hard to see any pros that compensate for the loss of affordability. The rise in rental rates and housing prices is not tied to any real improvement of the neighborhood. Local stores that once served all local residents are replaced by retail catering exclusively to the tastes of high-income households. Things are just more expensive. Nevertheless, the affordability measures I point to later in this chapter apply to these cases as well.

Additional complications stem from semantics. Opposing attitudes towards gentrification often have their basis in the fact that people have different things in mind when they use the term. For some, gentrification just means the involuntary displacement of low-income households. For that reason, they oppose it categorically. For others, it signifies re-investment in previously disinvested neighborhoods—dilapidated houses are rehabbed, vacant lots get new buildings, broken curbs are repaired, streetlights fixed. They are inclined to support it. Here I intend to distinguish between the two sides of the term and ask these questions: can we have re-investment without displacement? Can we have genuine neighborhood improvement without the loss of affordability? Can we, along with the Congress for the New Urbanism, support the "restoration of existing urban centers" without harming the poor?

Perhaps we can. One way to approach the problem of displacement is to encourage and build affordable housing close to public transit corridors. Affordable housing can be achieved in a number of ways. One is to allow for and build a mix of residential types—large, medium, and small—within the same neighborhood, from single-family detached to duplexes, townhouses, condominiums, and apartment buildings. Gently infilling existing neighborhoods with "missing middle" housing—residential types between single-family detached houses, on the one hand, and large apartment buildings on the other—will go part of the way to making homes more affordable for a wide range of incomes. Of special relevance are accessory dwelling units (ADUs), also known as "granny flats." Built in the back yard of a home, on top of a detached garage, or inside the primary residence, ADUs provide both rental income to the homeowner, making their homes more affordable, and reasonable rents to the occupants. That's a win-win proposition. Cities can promote ADUs by allowing them to be built by right rather than by special permission. Rent subsidies for very low to low income households are another piece of the puzzle. Supporting affordable mixed-income neighborhoods has the added social benefit of not concentrating poverty, disinvestment, and the lack of opportunity in an isolated area, thus raising the likelihood that all can live in safe neighborhoods with decent schools and adequate city services.

But housing costs are just one of two major factors when it comes to affordability. The other is transportation. Housing costs are relatively easy to calculate. They typically come in one monthly lump sum, either rent or mortgage payments (plus insurance and property taxes). Transportation costs are parceled out between car payments, insurance, taxes, depreciation, registration fees, gas, oil, tires, maintenance, and repairs. But when you add them up, they constitute a considerable sum. The average American household spends about 19 percent of its income on transportation.

In "location efficient" neighborhoods, walkable with public transit options, that portion goes down to just 9 percent. In auto-dependent exurbs, the number goes up to 25 percent. For very low income families in auto-dependent exurbs, the figure balloons to 55 percent and above.[5] In fact, in fifteen of the twenty-eight major metro areas studied by the Center of Housing Policy and the Center for Neighborhood Technology in 2005, working families with incomes between $20,000 and $50,000 a year spent as much or more on transportation than on housing.[6] That's why the Center for Transit-Oriented Development has created an affordability index that combines both housing and transportation costs.[7] In most cases, the greater the distance between the residential unit and public transit, the greater the transportation costs. The index shows that while housing may be less expensive in outlying areas, the associated transportation costs are typically higher. So there is often no real gain in affordability by moving out to the hinterlands. On the other hand, more expensive housing in a walkable neighborhood in town close to public transit may be more affordable. If a household can live with one less car, that fact alone, according to the American Automobile Association, represents an annual savings of some $8,700, which can be used for housing and other expenses.[8] For the purposes of affordable housing, neighborhood stability, and social equity, mixed housing neighborhoods are good. But mixed housing in walkable neighborhoods close to public transit is even better. It's called Transit-Oriented Development (TOD).

Public authorities at the city, county, state, and federal levels can make use of additional strategies to increase affordability and forestall the negative effects of gentrification.

There are basically two approaches: stimulate the production of affordable housing; or subsidize the "consumption" of housing. Under the subsidization category falls rent control and rent subsidies. Rent control caps the amount rent can rise on an annual basis. It is usually keyed to the consumer price index. For homeowners, the rise in property taxes can also be capped on a similar basis. Rent subsidies, like the federal Section Eight program, fills in the gap between the amount of the rent (the contract rent) and the ability to pay. Ability to pay is generally limited to 30 percent of gross income. Let's say the contract rent is $900 a month and a person makes $24,000 a year. The monthly amount of 30 percent of that income is $600. So $300 of federal Section Eight assistance then goes directly to the landlord to make up the difference. Home ownership can be made affordable in some cases through a creative combination of bank mortgages, grants from a city interested in reviving its tax base, and second mortgages extended by not-for-profit housing organizations.

The supply side is a little more complicated. The federal government can stimulate the production of affordable housing through state administered low-income housing tax credits (LIHTC). Typically, two thirds of the cost of a project are eligible for this kind of support. Let's say a developer has a $1.5 million project in mind. $1 million of the project serves as the eligible basis. If the developer offers an attractive package of affordable housing in the project, the government might award an LIHTC worth a 9 percent reduction in tax liabilities over ten years. On a project with a $1 million eligible basis, that's worth $900,000. A developer can then sell that LIHTC to an investor for a negotiated sum. The developer gets a wad of money for the project; the investor gets $900,000 in tax relief; and consumers get affordable housing—if they qualify. Who qualifies will be built into the developer's application for an LIHTC. The determination is usually made with reference to a percentage of area median income (AMI). So if a rental unit is to be affordable for households making 60 percent of AMI, and AMI is $60,000, the rent will be set at 30 percent of $36,000, which is $900.

A less complicated measure is the "density bonus" cities can offer to developers. Here the developer will be allowed to build additional units on a parcel of land, more than usually allowed, if the project includes a number of affordable units. That's a significant incentive. More rental units means more return on investment. Cities and counties can also mandate affordable housing through "inclusionary zoning," where 10 to 25 percent of the housing units in any new development over a certain size are required to be affordable. They can also assess a fee for any new development, where the fee goes into a housing trust fund for the support of affordable housing elsewhere in the city.

We live in a dynamic market economy. Neighborhoods change. A Serbian Eastern Orthodox church built years ago in Wicker Park—a neighborhood on the north side of Chicago—recently served a largely Hispanic congregation. Hamtramck, in the Detroit area, was once a predominantly Polish municipality; now it plays host to a significant number of families from Bangladesh and Yemen. In the early twentieth century, the Lower East Side of Manhattan was a largely Jewish neighborhood. It is no longer. The Baxter community of Grand Rapids, Michigan, was a Dutch immigrant neighborhood until the mid-twentieth century. Now it is predominantly African-American. But the number of Hispanic families in that neighborhood is growing. Ethnic and racial compositions shift. Property values wax and wane. Local cultures change. It would be both naive and unrealistic to think that neighborhoods can be frozen in time. We live in a dynamic market economy. But market forces should not be the only factors at work in shaping the cities and neighborhoods we live in. Through an open and inclusive process of democratic deliberation we should together decide on the kinds on communities we want to live in and the public policies that guide us in that direction. It's a matter of civic self-determination. The market economy is a powerful and proven engine of growth. But like any car, a city needs not only an engine but a steering wheel. We need to keep it from running over those of lesser means, the most vulnerable in gentrifying neighborhoods.

Neighborhoods in decline have their share of problems. Neighborhoods on the rebound have their share as well, chief among which is affordability. Yet a wide array of strategies can be used to keep housing affordable, even in neighborhoods that are experiencing gentrification. It is possible to promote re-investment in distressed neighborhoods and at the same time take the edge off involuntary displacement. But it takes a strong commitment, both public and private, to genuine community engagement and equitable development.

Notes

1. Edward Epstein and John Wildermuth, "Ammiano Pledges 'War' on Gentrification," *The San Francisco Chronicle*, November 18, 1999, A1.

2. Cindy Chang, "Boyle Heights activists protest art galleries, gentrification," *The Los Angeles Times*, November 5, 2016, http://www.latimes.com/local/lanow/la-me-ln-boyle-heights-protest-20161104-story.html.

3. We often think of gentrification as a matter of middle-class white folk moving into low-income black neighborhoods. But that need not be the case. The Chicago neighborhood of North Kenwood-Oakland, for instance, is gentrifying as middle-class African-American households move into a historically black neighborhood. See Brian McCabe, *No Place Like Home: Wealth, Community and the Politics of Homeownership* (Oxford: Oxford University Press, 2016), 108-109. Sometimes gentrification is the result of mostly high-income white households moving into middle-income white neighborhoods, as seen in the Del Ray neighborhood of Alexandria, Virginia—the spill-over effect of Washington, DC. Gentrification is primarily an economic issue.

4. Quoted in Sarah Hughes, "South Bronx: Home of Hip-Hop Fights to Keep its Soul as Gentrification Creeps In," *The Guardian*, August 13, 2016, https://www.theguardian.com/us-news/2016/aug/13/south-bronx-hip-hop-gentrification-the-get-down. Ms. Carter is a proponent of "self-gentrification," the improvement of a neighborhood by the people who already live there.

5. Center for Transit-Oriented Development, "Mixed-Income Housing Near Transit: Increasing Affordability with Local Efficiency," September 2009, 5, http://www.reconnectingamerica.org/assets/Uploads/091030ra-201mixedhousefinal.pdf.

6. "Mixed-Income Housing Near Transit," 4. See also the National Housing Conference study at nhc.org/index/heavyload.

7. See the Housing and Transportation Affordability index at htaindex.org.

8. This cost is according to an April 28, 2015 news release from the American Automobile Association (AAA), assuming the ownership of a typical sedan putting on 15,000 miles a year. The exact average cost is $8,698. See Erin Stepp, "Annual Cost to Own and Operate a Motor Vehicle Falls to $8,698, Finds AAA," April 28, 2015, http://newsroom.aaa.com/2015/04/annual-cost-operate-vehicle-falls-8698-finds-aaa-archive/.

Chapter 16

Where Is the Church?

I AM NOT a Catholic. But I know that I live in the St. Thomas the Apostle parish of the Catholic Church in Grand Rapids. Sunday mornings I see neighborhood families walking to 9:00 Mass, just two blocks away. On weekdays I see the school children in their uniforms walking to the Catholic parochial school next to the church. During the lunch hour they play in the neighborhood park next to the school, a shared use arrangement between the school and the city. On election days I walk over to their gym, which is my precinct's polling station. Once a year the church holds a recycling program in its parking lot for big-ticket items. Every day of the year, the church sanctuary remains open to all for prayer. I am not a Catholic. But I think there is much to admire in the Catholic parish system. The churches are embedded in the neighborhoods they serve. And they serve their neighborhoods in many ways. At their best, they represent a stable and accessible redemptive presence in that part of the world they've been given to inhabit.

As a rule, Protestant churches are not bound by an official parish system. They serve a particular population rather than a particular place. They need not stay put. Prior to the Second World War, many of them presided over de facto parishes—immigrant neighborhoods in the city where we might find, for example, a German Lutheran church serving a predominantly German neighborhood. But after the war, with the scattering of the tribes throughout suburbia, access to the church was increasingly defined by mobility rather than proximity. Since the 1950s, many Protestant churches have abandoned city neighborhoods altogether and followed their congregants out to the suburbs and even the uttermost parts of the exurbs. Out on the edge, in the exurban setting, churches typically locate on arterials between land use pods and surround themselves with huge parking lots to accommodate their members who come by car from distant points over a large region. In a built environment where cars are the only way to get around, they are well aware of the number one rule of church growth: a church will never get bigger than its parking lot.[1] Some have even achieved the enviable status of a megachurch with a weekly attendance of over 2,000.

Typologically, exurban edge churches are modeled on the regional shopping mall. While much good is often done in the ministries of these churches, their location and their relation to the built environment carry certain implications—and limitations. For one, such churches are accessible only by car. As we noted earlier, one third of the American population does not drive. Exurban church location presents a special challenge to our most vulnerable populations: those too young, too old, too infirm, or too poor to own and operate an automobile.

The isolated church campus in the car-dependent culture of the exurbs also means that, for the most part, people come into contact with the church only when they go there as a matter of explicit intention. Gone are the serendipitous encounters in the immediate neighborhood and the casual visits by curious passersby. It's ministry by appointment.

Because of their civic isolation, such churches tend to draw their congregants not by their inviting physical presence and immediate community involvement, but by their specialized programming, high production-value worship performances, and pastor personality. Self-selection for those congregations on the basis of taste and preference tends to reduce real diversity. They more often engage in niche ministries (young adult groups, divorcee groups, bereaved groups, retiree groups, or medical support groups for various aliments) than place-based ministries (food pantries, after-school tutoring programs, or neighborhood youth clubs). Some may try to become place-based centers of community by including gyms, bowling alleys, coffee shops, skateboard parks, and performance space on their campus. But these are private lifestyle enclaves, places where believers of certain stripe can have fun together in a safe and insular environment. Because of the lack of a concrete connection to their immediate surroundings, congregational mission efforts often turn to organizing short-term mission trips to far off places, where lay members encounter people they don't know in cultures they don't understand for periods of time too short to get anything of much significance done.[2] It's hard to bloom where you're planted when there's no where there.

Consider, by contrast, churches situated in an existing community. Although churches embedded in traditional neighborhoods can be lifeless, financially strapped, and lacking in vision, their location and their relation to the built

environment also carry certain implications—and opportunities. They find themselves in the midst of a larger civic
community. They tend to be more accessible by a wider
array of transit modes (pedestrian, bike, bus, subway, light
rail, as well as car). Their location keeps the liturgical gathering point in the neighborhood where congregants actually
live, move, and have a good deal of their being. Members
are more likely to see and support each other throughout
the week, which makes for a stronger faith community.
Moreover, such churches are in a position to draw both the
committed and the curious on the basis of proximity and
community engagement, which can make for more real-life
diversity and balance out their congregations and ministries.

Take the case of Sara Miles, a journalist living in the
Mission District of San Francisco. She was in the habit of
taking long walks through her neighborhood.

> Early one morning, when Katie [her daughter] was sleeping
> at her father's house, I walked into St. Gregory's Episcopal
> Church in San Francisco. I had no earthly reason to be there.
> I'd never heard a Gospel reading, never said the Lord's Prayer.
> I was certainly not interested in becoming a Christian—or, as
> I thought of it rather less politely, a religious nut. But on other
> long walks, I'd passed the beautiful wooden building, with its
> shingled steeples and plain windows, and this time I went in, on
> an impulse, with no more than a reporter's habitual curiosity.[3]

She participated in communion and was palpably transformed in that moment, only later to learn what it was all
about. She set up a food pantry at the church, which now
serves over 1,200 families. Today she continues to write—and
works as the director of ministry at St. Gregory's.

Even if a majority of their members are commuters, embedded churches can play a healing role in the neighborhoods they inhabit though place-based ministries. In addition, they are often able to provide a civic focal point, a civic anchor, for their surrounding communities. It is not unusual for them to serve as a meeting place for neighborhood associations, senior centers, public lectures, concerts, police contacts with the community, interactions with city commissioners, presentations by developers, distribution points for food, community health clinics, exercise programs, and the like. Some offer weekday child care. Some run small bookstores and coffee shops. The neighborhood is their campus.

How shall we judge between these two models, the edge church and the embedded church? The first thing we should say is that churches, like individuals, can have different callings. Just as we hold that individuals have different gifts and therefore different roles to play in the body of Christ, so too we might hold that churches have different gifts and therefore different roles to play in the ministry of the body of Christ. Perhaps every metropolitan area should have a regional megachurch or two in addition to neighborhood churches. Exurban areas need to be served. The problem is that regional megachurches have in many cases become the ideal to which other churches aspire, motivating neighborhood churches to move out to the edge of town in the search of cheap land, larger parking lots, and a regional catchment.

Even if neighborhood churches don't move out to the edge, often their members do. Eighty percent of megachurch growth is fueled by church transfers, not conversions,[4] thus drawing congregants out of their immediate communities and creating even more of a disconnect between where they live and where they worship. This is unfortunate, in my view. In the incarnation, God practiced the ministry of presence. "Incarnation" means, quite literally, taking on flesh, being physically present—coming up close to where people live, especially the most vulnerable. Should the community of those who follow the Incarnate One do otherwise? Perhaps the civically isolated megachurch should be the exception rather than the rule.

Lesslie Newbigin, English missionary and theologian, lamented the loss of the parish in the life of the church. Without a tether to place and a placed-based sense of mission, with more attention given to growth in membership numbers and relative market share, Christian churches often give a sorry impression to those who would observe them.

> Their picture of the Church is of a series of competing congregations, each of which is a sort of religious club catering to the religious tastes of its members. The aim of each congregation is to attract as many members as possible to its services, increase its income and improve its buildings. . . . The game is a "free for all" and everyone is at liberty to join in the scramble for membership. Each congregation is simply concerned for its own aggrandizement and there is no sense of responsibility for the welfare of society as a whole. The whole concept of the "parish" is completely lost.[5]

A harsh judgment indeed. Perhaps overly harsh. But it may serve the purpose of suggesting an alternative vision of Christian ministry and mission, where the parish comes back into view and the mission of the church becomes less self-regarding and more focused on the common good. The alternative finds succinct expression in the work of Timothy Keller, until recently the senior pastor of Redeemer Presbyterian Church in New York City. By its numbers, Redeemer could be considered a megachurch. It draws over 5,000 attendees to its services each week (even though it doesn't have a parking lot). But the spirit is different. "Christians," Keller writes, "should seek to live in the city, not to use the city to build great churches, but to use the resources of the church to seek a great, flourishing city. We refer to this as a 'city growth' model of ministry rather than a strictly 'church growth' model."[6] On this model, churches are "looking for ways to strengthen the health of their neighborhoods, making them safer and more humane places to live. This is a way to seek the welfare of the city, in the spirit of Jeremiah 29."[7] Members of churches, "work for the peace, security, justice, and prosperity of their neighbors, loving them in word and deed, whether or not they believe the same things we believe in."[8]

To better serve the neighborhoods of its parishioners, and to avoid undue focus on a singular pastor, Redeemer has decided to get smaller rather than bigger. It subdivided into three locations in Manhattan—the West Side, the East Side, and Downtown. The Urban Village Church in Chicago follows a similar approach when it comes to church growth. Rather than aspiring to become a large church in one location and expecting its members to leave their neighborhoods and travel miles by car to attend its services, it stays small, local, close, and embedded. It grows by replicating itself, neighborhood by neighborhood. With signal emphases on hospitality, justice, inclusion, service, and discipleship, it has established a vital presence in four Chicago neighborhoods—Hyde Park, South Loop, Wicker Park, and Andersonville—with the intent of growing by starting an additional local faith community in the Windy City every one to two years. Like Redeemer Presbyterian, it intends to grow by replication rather than expansion.

Clearly the ministry of the Word is central to the work of Redeemer. It is theologically conservative. And its members can find pastoral support for their personal struggles. But its sense of mission is defined by the urban context in which the church is situated. And if the church, as Newbigin puts it, is to function as the "first fruit, sign, and instrument of God's new creation," as a pilot plant for redemption and reconciliation, the urban context is in many ways ideal.[9] The city, Keller notes, is "humanity intensified—a magnifying glass that brings out the very best and the very worst of human nature."[10] The city is the site of diversity, contrast, and contest—racial, ethnic, social, economic, cultural, and intellectual.[11] It is, in addition, a center of cultural production—whether local, regional, national, or global. What better place for the community of faith to model, as best it can, the grace, hope, and reconciling power of the gospel? The city occupies a specific patch of ground where people unlike each other have to live together. What better crucible for the church to both learn from and contribute to the common good of the human community? "The question," writes Newbigin, "that has to be asked about the church and about every congregation is not: How big is it? How fast is it growing? How rich is it? It is: What difference is it making to that bit of the world in which it has been placed?"[12] Of course the Christian church should make a difference wherever it is located. But the city is an especially excellent bit of the world in which the Christian church can make a difference. A similar appreciation for the role of place in the mission and ministry of the church is displayed on the west coast in the New Parish movement coming out of Seattle. It had its origins in questioning the megachurch model of the church as an out-sized affinity group located on the edge of town. There, write the authors of *The New Parish*, "churches drew people out of the diversity of their own neighborhood contexts; . . . in a homogenous gathering, they would 'consume' a worship event crafted with excellence appealing to a specific audience."[13] Instead, New Parish churches focus on establishing a "faithful presence" in existing neighborhoods with their diverse demographics and cultural mix,[14] where the primary mission is devoted to the work of the "commons"—to what we share with others in the areas of education, civic life, economic activity, and the natural environment.[15] The faithful presence of a church, then, means to seek a flourishing life for all within a given place.[16] Its civic role is more a matter of inhabiting a place than issue advocacy, which runs the risk of reducing the church to another special interest group in the politics of the culture wars.[17] The emphasis is on self-giving service, not political dominance. "A theology of faithful presence first calls Christians to attend to the people and places that they experience directly," writes James Davison Hunter in *To Change the World*.[18]

> Faithful presence gives priority to what is right in front of us—the community, the neighborhood, and the city, and the people of which these are constituted. For most, this will mean a preference for stability, locality, and particularity of place and its needs. It is here, through the joys, sufferings, hopes,

disappointments, concerns, desires, and worries of the people
with whom we are in long-term and close relation—family,
neighbors, coworkers, and community—where we find our
authenticity as a body and as believers.[19]

In addition, New Parish churches place less trust in the
latest strategies for church growth, market techniques,
ministry formulas, or, more generally, any standardized
method for achieving outcomes we envision for ourselves.
The emphasis, rather, is on paying attention to the unique
features of a context, observing how the Spirit is at work in
a particular place, and then falling in line with that work.[20]
Cooperation is the key, not control. "This approach is a much
more fruitful means of learning than centralized planning
where experts offer top-down procedures that transcend
the contextual dynamics of time and place."[21] The approach
should sound familiar: like Jane Jacobs, New Parish churches
are committed to the open and patient process of appreciative inquiry, this time prompted by the Spirit.

Although Protestant churches have been fragmented
into many different denominations, they can find unity in
a common mission of place if not in the finer points of their
theological positions. Consider True City, a collaboration of
sixteen churches in the Canadian city of Hamilton, Ontario.
Working under the banner "churches together for the good
of the city," True City promotes education by providing back-
packs and school supplies to over 1,000 children each fall,
builds up civil society by holding fundraising events for local
charities, supports refugees, prepares food hampers for families at Christmas, fosters communication and collaboration
between the member churches, sponsors art exhibits and

concerts, supports urban gardens, and engages in cooper-
ative youth programming. In their vision statement, they
point to the fact that their member congregations

> are increasingly identifying and engaging with their neighbor-
> hood. They are open and welcoming to everyone, and involved
> in many aspects of the life of the neighborhood. They serve
> others sacrificially and generously, and allow themselves to be
> served and shaped by the experiences and insights of others.
> These congregations are cultivating community around prac-
> tices of Word and Sacrament and indwelling the story of God's
> redemptive and loving involvement in the world. Emphasizing
> presence over program, they are the local embodiments of
> God's reign and mission in this city.[22]

The extended vision statement of True City is worth quot-
ing at some length as it captures many of the themes central
to the Christian church's rediscovery of locality and the rich
missional opportunities presented by the urban context:

> Vital congregations are spreading across the city and contrib-
> uting to the public good. In each neighborhood, congregations
> are coming alongside people on the margins and at risk, such
> as: single parents, at risk children and teens, mental illness
> survivors, the elderly, immigrants and refugees. They are also
> coming alongside to strengthen the work of local institutions
> and initiatives like: schools, neighborhood associations, and
> community centres. Christians who understand their missional
> vocation are catalysts for positive change in education, the
> marketplace, the arts and other areas of civic life.[23]

As a result, True City churches in Hamilton observe that
in their areas of influence,

fewer people are resorting to criminal, self-destructive behavior, and poverty is becoming less prevalent. There is sustainable economic growth; meaningful employment; a sustainable, healthy economy; a beautiful environment (both natural and constructed); just wages; quality consumer products; and stable, expanding employment. It is becoming increasingly clear in people's minds that the presence of the people of God in this city is contributing to the universal flourishing of Hamilton.[24]

Hamilton could be considered the Pittsburgh of Canada. A city of about 500,000 souls, its economy was largely based on the steel industry on the southern shore of Lake Ontario. With the collapse of that industry in the 1980s and the departure of several major employers like Westinghouse, International Harvester, and Proctor and Gamble, the city—especially the east side—fell prey to the familiar urban problems of disinvestment, unemployment, poverty, drugs, crime, homelessness, and prostitution. Several members of the Compass Point Bible Church in the Hamilton area wondered how they could help turn things around. They began not with big ideas, but by simply observing the situation with a prayerful eye. The standard options of setting up a food pantry or soup kitchen didn't seem right. They might help patch the symptoms, but they wouldn't get close to the source of the problems. The neighborhood, they noted, had its fair share of bars and fast food joints. Yet something was missing. They decided to establish a third place in the form of a cafe with a menu of real food at affordable prices in a family-friendly environment.

Thus was born 541 Eatery and Exchange, a neighborhood cafe—and much more—in a former bank building at 541 Barton Street. Run by a small paid staff, the day-to-day work is largely done by a force of some two hundred volunteers. The physical space, much of the volunteer time, and the proceeds go to supporting free educational initiatives for the community as well as a variety of local groups: a homework club, meetings for moms with autistic kids, a writers group, a book club, classes in kitchen skills and barista skills, piano keyboard lessons, and workshops in nutrition. The Meeting Place congregation gathers there for worship on Sunday afternoons, sharing a meal afterwards. Thus 541 seeks to establish itself as a hub of hope in an environment filled with much despair. It holds special fundraising dinners and runs teen leadership camps, where high-school-age kids learn leadership and job skills while working side-by-side with volunteers at the Eatery. Soon they will open a community kitchen, supported by a catering contract, several doors down the street.

As a third place, 541 provides a venue for the exchange of ideas and stories, dialogue and counsel. It has also set up a simple mechanism where those of means can easily share with those in need. If you visit the shop, you will note a jar full of buttons on the counter. The jar gives customers an opportunity to pay it forward. Buy a button for a dollar and put it in the jar. Others can use the buttons to pay for their meals as they have need (up to five buttons a day per person).[25] 541 is one of many fine examples of what can happen when people of faith and good will turn their attention to the needs and resources of their own communities. It's not about short-term mission trips to far off places; it's about faithful presence at home over the long haul.

The built environment can at best provide us with a fitting stage for human life and positive forms of civic involvement, social interaction, and mutual support. But just as a great stage cannot guarantee a good performance, so the finest of urban structures cannot not guarantee a well-functioning human community. It is up to us to play our roles—investing our time and energy in human relations and civic institutions. "Ultimately," writes Mark Mitchell, a political theorist at Patrick Henry College, "healthy communities will only be realized when individuals commit to a particular place and to particular neighbors in the long-term work of making a place, or recognizing and enjoying the responsibilities and pleasures of membership in a local community."[26] Many of those responsibilities and pleasures of membership will involve acts of restoration, including the restoration of our built environment. So much of our landscape has already been ruined by ill-considered development.

In Abraham Verghese's fine novel *Cutting for Stone*, the fictive narrator, Marion Stone, speaks of his twin brother, Shiva. They had been born in Ethiopia of a secret union between an Indian Carmelite nun and a brash but brilliant British surgeon. Their mother died in childbirth; their father summarily disowned them. Both, nonetheless, turned to their father's profession later in life. They became surgeons. Shiva specialized in the repair of fistulas—unauthorized tunnels that develop between adjacent organs. "According to Shiva," Marion noted, "life is in the end about fixing holes. Shiva didn't speak in metaphors. Fixing holes is precisely what he did." Yet fixing holes can serve as a metaphor for our life's work. And Marion makes use of it. "We are all fixing what is broken. It is the task of a lifetime. We'll leave much unfinished for the next generation."[27]

Fixing holes. Fixing what is broken. The repair of creation. This is indeed the work of a lifetime. And the fixing of our built environment—the wise redevelopment of our cities, the retro-fitting of our suburbs, the reconfiguration of dead malls, the re-design of our streets, the multiplication of transit options, and the creation of fine and fitting public places for the support of civic life—surely this will be the work of several generations.

Notes

1. Os Guinness, *Dining with the Devil: The Megachurch Movement Flirts with the Devil* (Grand Rapids: Baker Book House, 1993), 38.

2. See Omni Elisha, *Moral Ambition: Mobilization and Social Outreach in Evangelical Megachurches* (Berkeley: University of California Press, 2011); Robert D. Lupton, *Toxic Charity: How Churches and Charites Hurt Those They Help, and How to Reverse It* (New York: Harper One, 2012), and Justin G. Wilford, *Sacred Subdivisions: The Postsuburban Transformation of American Evangelicalism* (New York: New York University Press, 2012), especially 128-34.

3. Sarah Miles, *Take this Bread: A Radical Conversion* (New York: Ballantine Books: 2007), 5. See also https://sara-miles.squarespace.com/ and TheFoodPantry.org.

4. Guinness, *Dining with the Devil*, 78.

5. Lesslie Newbigin, "The Role of the Parish in Society," in *The Good Shepherd Meditations on Christian Ministry in Today's World* (Grand Rapids: Eerdmans, 1977), 86.

6. Timothy Keller, *Center Church* (Grand Rapids: Zondervan, 2012), 172.

7. Keller, *Center Church*, 175.

8. Keller, *Center Church*, 171.

9. Newbigin, "The Role of the Parish," 88.

10. Keller, *Center Church*, 135.

11. Keller, *Center Church*, 171.

12. Newbigin, "The Role of the Parish," 88.

13. Paul Sparks, Tim Soerens, and Dwight J. Friesen, *The New Parish: How Neighborhood Churches are Transforming Mission, Discipleship, and Community* (Downers Grove. IL: InterVarsity, 2014), 44.

14. Sparks, Soerens, and Friesen, *The New Parish*, 46.

15. Sparks, Soerens, and Friesen, *The New Parish*, 95-96.

16. Sparks, Soerens, and Friesen, *The New Parish*, 47.

17. Sparks, Soerens, and Friesen, *The New Parish*, 111.

18. James Davison Hunter, *To Change the World: The Irony, Tragedy, and Possibility of Christianity in the Late Modern World* (Oxford: Oxford University Press, 2010), 253.

19. Hunter, *To Change the World*, 253.

20. Sparks, Soerens, and Friesen, *The New Parish*, 62.

21. Sparks, Soerens, and Friesen, *The New Parish*, 159.

22. True City, Hamilton, "Vision," 2017, http://truecityhamilton.ca/about/vision/. British spelling Americanized.

23. True City, Hamilton, "Vision."

24. True City, Hamilton, "Vision."

25. For information on 541 Eatery and Exchange, see fivefortyone.ca.

26. Mark T. Mitchell, "Wendell Berry and the New Urbanism: Agrarian Remedies, Urban Prospects," in *Front Porch Republic*, March 20, 2011, http://www.frontporchrepublic.com/2011/03/wendell-berrys-new-urbanism-agrarian-remedies-urban-prospects/, quoted in Keller, *Center Church*, 171.

27. Abraham Verghese, *Cutting for Stone* (New York: Random House, 2009), 9.

Resources

Recommended Reading

Each chapter of this book is a mini-essay on a topic that would easily admit of book-length treatment. Those interested in additional readings on urbanism and urban design would do well to start with the following books.

For a more extensive overview of urbanism and urban design:

Duany, Andres, Elizabeth Plater-Zyberk, and Jeff Speck. *Suburban Nation: The Rise of Sprawl and the Decline of the American Dream.* New York: North Point, 2000; second edition, 2010.

Gehl, Jan. *Cities for People.* Washington, DC: Island Press, 2010.

Jacobs, Jane. *The Death and Life of Great American Cities.* New York: Random House; Vintage Books, 1992.

Kunstler, James Howard. *The Geography of Nowhere: The Rise and Decline of America's Man-Made Landscape.* New York: Free Press, 1994.

Speck, Jeff. *Walkable City: How Downtown Can Save America, One Step at a Time.* New York: Farrer, Straus and Giroux, 2012.

For a history of Anglo-American cities and suburbanization:

Fishman, Robert. *Bourgeois Utopias: The Rise and Fall of Suburbia.* New York: Basic Books, 1987.

Hayden, Delores. *Building Suburbia: Green Fields and Urban Growth, 1820-2000.* New York: Vintage Books, 2004.

Jackson, Kenneth T. *Crabgrass Frontier: The Suburbanization of the United States.* New York: Oxford University Press, 1985.

On race, class, and housing segregation:

McCabe, Brian J. *No Place Like Home: Wealth, Community and the Politics of Homeownership.* Oxford: Oxford University Press, 2016.
Reeves, Richard V. *Dream Hoarders: How the American Upper Middle Class is Leaving Everyone Else in the Dust, Why That is a Problem, and What to Do About It.* Washington, DC: Brookings Institution Press, 2017.
Rothstein, Richard. *The Color of Law: A Forgotten History of How Our Government Segregated America.* New York: Liverlight Publishing Company, 2017.

On urbanism and the environment:

Farr, Douglas. *Sustainable Urbanism: Urban Design with Nature.* Hoboken, NJ: John Wiley & Sons, 2007.
Mouzon, Stephen A. *The Original Green: Unlocking the Mystery of True Sustainability.* Miami: Guild Foundation, 2010.
Owen, David. *Green Metropolis: Why Living Smaller, Living Closer, and Driving Less are the Keys to Sustainability.* New York: Riverhead, 2009.

On cars and streets:

Dover, Victor and John Massengale. *Street Design: The Secret to Great Cities and Towns.* Hoboken, NJ: Wiley, 2014.
Jacobs, Allen. *Great Streets.* Cambridge: MIT Press, 1995.
Kay, Jane Holtz. *Asphalt Nation: How the Automobile Took Over America, and How We Can Take It Back.* Berkeley: University of California, 1997.

On sprawl and civic engagement:

Williamson, Thad. *Sprawl, Justice, and Citizenship: The Civic Cost of the American Way of Life.* Oxford: Oxford University Press, 2010.

On theology, church, and urbanism:

Bartholomew, Craig G. *Where Mortals Dwell: A Christian View of Place for Today*. Grand Rapids: Baker Academic: 2011.

Benesh, Sean. *Blueprints for a Just City: The Role of the Church in Urban Planning and Shaping the City's Built Environment*. Portland, OR: Urban Loft Publishers, 2015.

Bess, Phillip. *Till We Have Built Jerusalem: Architecture, Urbanism, and the Sacred*. Wilmington: Intercollegiate Studies Institute, 2006.

Gorringe, T. J. *A Theology of the Built Environment*. Cambridge: Cambridge University Press, 2002.

Hjalmarson, Leonard. *No Home Like Place: A Christian Theology of Place*. Portland, OR: Urban Loft Publishers, 2104.

Jacobsen, Eric. *Sidewalks in the Kingdom: New Urbanism and the Christian Faith*. Grand Rapids: Brazos, 2003.

_____. *The Space Between: A Christian Engagement with the Built Environment*. Grand Rapids: Baker Academic, 2012.

Keller, Timothy. *Center Church*. Grand Rapids: Zondervan, 2012.

Sparks, Paul, Tim Soerens, and Dwight Friesen. *The New Parish: How Neighborhood Churches are Transforming Mission, Discipleship, and Community*. Downers Grove, IL: InterVarsity Press, 2014.

Toly, Noah J. *Cities of Tomorrow and the City to Come: A Theology of Urban Life*. Grand Rapids, MI: Zondervan, 2015.

Web Resources

Urbanism, Urban Design, Urban Planning:

The Congress for the New Urbanism (CNU): cnu.org
Smart Growth: smartgrowthamerica.org
Build a Better Burb: buildabetterburb.org
Project for Public Spaces (PPS): pps.org
Strong Towns: strongtowns.org
AARP / Livable Communities: aarp.org/livable-communities
The Atlantic / CityLab: citylab.com

Next City / Inspiring Better Cities: nextcity.org
Places / A Public Journal on Architecture, Landscape, and Urbanism: placesjournal.org
Planetizen / For people passionate about planning: planetizen.com
The City Observatory: cityobservatory.org
New Urbanism Film Festival: newurbanismfilmfestival.com
American Makeover Series: youtube.com, search "American Makeover."
Walkscore / Rate the walkability of your residence: walkscore.com

Form-based codes:

Form-Based Codes: formbasedcodes.org
Center for Applied Transect Studies: transect.org

Streets and Transit:

Complete Streets: completestreets.org
Bicycle Infrastructure: nacto.org
Transit-Oriented Development: reconnectingamerica.org
StreetsBlog / To improve walking, biking, and transit: streetsblog.org
Street Films / Livable Streets Videos: streetfilms.org

Affordable housing:

Missing Middle Housing: missingmiddlehousing.com
Accessory Dwelling Units: accessorydwellings.org

Church, Neighborhoods, and the Commons:

New City Commons: newcitycommons.org
Redeemer Presbyterian Church NYC: redeemer.com
City to City: redeemercitytocity.com
Urban Village Church: urbanvillagechurch.org
The New Parish Movement: parishcollective.org, theseattleschool.edu
True City Hamilton: truecityhamilton.ca
541 Eatery and Exchange: fivefortyone.ca

Bibliography

Alexander, T. Desmond. *From Paradise to Promised Land: An Introduction to the Pentateuch*. Grand Rapids: Baker Academic, 2012.

Badger, Emily. "The Simple Math that Can Save Cities from Bankruptcy." *Atlantic Cities*, March 30, 2012, https://www.citylab.com/life/2012/03/simple-math-can-save-cities-bankruptcy/1629/.

Bartholomew, Craig G. *Where Mortals Dwell: A Christian View of Place Today*. Grand Rapids: Baker Academic, 2011.

Beecher, Catherine. *A Treatise on Domestic Economy for the Use of Young Ladies at Home and at School*. Rev. ed. New York: Harper and Brothers, 1855.

Benesh, Sean. *Blueprints for a Just City: The Role of the Church in Urban Planning and Shaping the City's Built Environment*. Portland, OR: Urban Loft Publishers, 2015.

Bess, Philip. *Till We Have Built Jerusalem: Architecture, Urbanism, and the Sacred*. Wilmington: ISI Books, 2006.

Bishop, Bill. *The Big Sort: Why the Clustering of Like-Minded America is Tearing Us Apart*. New York: Houghton Mifflin, 2008.

Brain, David. "From Good Neighborhoods to Sustainable Cities." *International Regional Science Review*, 28 (2005): 217–38.

Catechism of the Catholic Church. New York: Doubleday, 1995.

Centers for Disease Control and Prevention (CDC). Motor Vehicle Safety. "Teen Drivers: Get the Facts." October 16, 2016. www.cdc.gov/MotorVehicleSafety/Teen_Drivers/teendrivers_factsheet.html.

Center for Transit-Oriented Development. "Mixed-Income Housing Near Transit: Increasing Affordability with Local Efficiency." September 2009. http://www.reconnectingamerica.org/assets/Uploads/091030ra-201mixedhousefinal.pdf.

Chang, Cindy. "Boyle Heights activists protest art galleries, gentrification." *The Los Angeles Times*, November 5, 2016. http://www.latimes.com/local/lanow/la-me-ln-boyle-heights-protest-20161104-story.html.

Conn, Steven. *Americans against the City: Anti-Urbanism in the Twentieth Century*. Oxford: Oxford University Press, 2014.

Cowper, William. *The Task, A Poem in Six Books*. London: J. Johnson, 1785.

Dahl, Darren. "Why Downtown Development May be More Affordable than the Suburbs." *Forbes*, March 14, 2014, https://www.forbes.com/sites/citi/2014/03/14/why-downtown-development-may-be-more-affordable-than-the-suburbs/#137ff8a55bde.

de Tocqueville, Alexis. *Democracy in America*. New York: Harper and Row, 1969.

Downing, Andrew Jackson. *Rural Essays*. Edited by George William Curtis. New York: G. P. Putnam, 1853.

_____. *Victorian Cottage Residences*. New York: Dover Publications, 1981. A republication of the 5th ed., John Wiley and Son, 1873. First published in 1842 under the title *Cottage Residences*.

Duany, Andres, Elizabeth Plater-Zyberk, and Jeff Speck. *Suburban Nation: The Rise of Sprawl and the Decline of the American Dream*. New York: North Point, 2000.

Duany, Andres, Jeff Speck, and Mike Lydon. *The Smart Growth Manual*. New York: McGraw-Hill, 2010.

Durning, Alan Thein. *The Car and the City*. Seattle: Northwest Environment Watch, 1996.

Ehrenhalt, Alan. *The Great Inversion and the Future of the American City*. New York: Random House, 2012.

Elisha, Omni. *Moral Ambition: Mobilization and Social Outreach in Evangelical Megachurches*. Berkeley: University of California Press, 2011.

Elliott, Debbie. "One of America's Longest-Serving Mayors Steps Down." *NPR Weekend Edition Saturday*, January 9, 2016. http://www.npr.org/2016/01/09/462400074/americas-longest-serving-mayor-steps-down.

Epstein, Edward, and John Wildermuth, "Ammiano Pledges 'War' on Gentrification." *The San Francisco Chronicle*, November 18, 1999, A1.

Epstein, Jim, and Nick Gillespie. "The Tragedy of Urban Renewal: The destruction and survival of a New York City neighborhood." Reason.

com. September 28, 2011. http://reason.com/blog/2011/09/28/the-tragedy-of-urban-renewal-t.

Ewing, Reid, Keith Bartholomew, Steve Winkelman, Jerry Walters, and Don Chen. *Growing Cooler: Evidence on Urban Development and Climate Change.* Washington, DC: Urban Land Institute, 2008.

Ewing, Reid, and Eric Dumbaugh. "The Built Environment and Traffic Safety: A Review of the Evidence." *Journal of Planning Literature* 23, no. 4 (May, 2009): 347-367.

Ewing, Reid, Tom Schmid, Richard Killingsworth, Amy Zlot, and Stephen Raudenbush. "Relationship between Urban Sprawl and Physical Activity, Obesity, and Morbidity." *American Journal of Health Promotion.* 18, no. 1 (September/October 2003): 47–57.

FBI Unified Crime Report, www.fbi.gov/about-us/cjis/ucr.

Fishman, Robert. *Bourgeois Utopias: The Rise and Fall of Suburbia.* New York: Basic Books, 1987.

Flint, Anthony. *Wrestling with Moses: How Jane Jacobs Took on New York's Master Builder and Transformed the American City.* New York: Random House, 2011.

Freeman, Lance. *There Goes the 'Hood: Views of Gentrification from the Ground Up.* Philadelphia: Temple University Press, 2006.

Fulton, William, et al. *Building Better Budgets: A National Examination of the Fiscal Benefits of Smart Growth Development.* Smart Growth America, 2013.

Gorringe, T. J. *A Theology of the Built Environment.* Cambridge: Cambridge University Press, 2002.

Guinness, Os. *Dining with the Devil: The Megachurch Movement Flirts with Modernity.* Grand Rapids: Baker, 1993.

Hayden, Delores. *Redesigning the American Dream.* New York: Norton, 2002.

Hilberseimer, Ludwig. *The New City: Principles of Planning.* Chicago: Paul Theobald, 1944.

Hjalmarson, Leonard. *No Home Like Place: A Christian Theology of Place.* Portland, OR: Urban Loft Publishers, 2104.

Holmes, Steven A. "Fannie Mae Eases Credit to Aid Mortgage Lending." *The New York Times,* September 30, 1999. http://www.nytimes.com/1999/09/30/business/fannie-mae-eases-credit-to-aid-mortgage-lending.html.

Holtzclaw, John, Robert Clear, Hank Dittmar, David Goldstein, and Peter

Haas. "Location Efficiency: Neighborhood and Socio-economic characteristics determine auto ownership and use studies in Chicago, Los Angeles and San Francisco." *Transportation Planning Technology* 25, no. 1 (2002): 1-27.

Hughes, Sarah. "South Bronx: Home of Hip-Hop Fights to Keep its Soul as Gentrification Creeps In." *The Guardian*, August 13, 2016. https://www.theguardian.com/us-news/2016/aug/13/south-bronx-hip-hop-gentrification-the-get-down.

Hunter, James Davison. *To Change the World: The Irony, Tragedy, and Possibility of Christianity in the Late Modern World.* Oxford: Oxford University Press, 2010.

Jackson, Kenneth. *Crabgrass Frontier: The Suburbanization of the United States.* New York: Oxford University Press, 1985.

Jacobs, Jane. *The Death and Life of Great American Cities.* New York: Random House, 1961.

_____. "Downtown is for People." *Fortune*, 57, no. 4 (April 1958): 133-40, 236–42.

Jacobsen, Eric. *Sidewalks in the Kingdom: New Urbanism and the Christian Faith.* Grand Rapids: Brazos, 2003.

_____. *The Space Between: A Christian Engagement with the Built Environment.* Grand Rapids: Baker Academic, 2012.

Kay, Jane Holtz. *Asphalt Nation: How the Automobile Took over America and How We Can Take It Back.* Berkeley: University of California Press, 1997.

Keller, Timothy. *Center Church.* Grand Rapids: Zondervan, 2012.

Killingsworth, Richard E. , and Jean Lamming. "Could our development patterns be affecting our personal health?" *Development and Public Health*, Local Government Commission, July 13, 2013, lgc.org/ development-public-health.

Kunstler, James Howard. *The Geography of Nowhere.* New York: Simon and Schuster, 1993.

_____. *Home from Nowhere.* New York: Simon and Schuster, 1996.

_____. "Home from Nowhere." *The Atlantic Monthly* 278, no. 3 (September, 1996): 43-66.

Le Corbusier. *The City of Tomorrow and Its Planning.* New York: Dover Publications, 1987; a reprint of the English edition originally published by Payson and Clarke, 1929. Translation of *Urbanisme*. Paris: G. Cres & Cie, 1924 .

————. *The Radiant City*. New York: Orion, 1967. Translation of *La Ville Radieuse*. Paris: Vincent, Freal, and Cie, 1933.

Leyden, Kevin M. "Social Capital and the Built Environment: The Importance of Walkable Neighborhoods." *American Journal of Public Health*, 93, no. 9 (September 2003):1546–51.

Lopez, Russ P. "Public Health, the APHA, and Urban Renewal." *American Journal of Public Health*, 99, no. 9 (September 2009): 1603–11.

Lucy, William. "Mortality Risk Associated with Leaving Home: Recognizing the Relevance of the Built Environment." *American Journal of Public Health*, 93, no. 9 (September 2003): 1564–69.

Lucy, William and Raphael Rabelais. "Traffic Fatalities and Homicides by Strangers: Danger of Leaving Home in Cities, Inner Suburbs, and Outer Suburbs." Unpublished manuscript, University of Virginia. April, 2002.

Lupton, Robert D. *Toxic Charity: How Churches and Charites Hurt Those They Help, and How to Reverse It*. New York: Harper One, 2012.

McCabe, Brian J. *No Place Like Home: Wealth, Community and the Politics of Homeownership*. Oxford: Oxford University Press, 2016.

Miles, Sarah. *Take this Bread: A Radical Conversion*. New York: Ballantine Books: 2007.

————. *City of God: Faith in the Streets*. New York: Jericho Books, 2014.

Minicozzi, Joe. "The Smart Math of Mixed Use Development." *Planetizen*, January 23, 2012, https://www.planetizen.com/node/53922.

————. "Thinking Differently about Development." *Government Finance Review*, August, 2013: 44-48.

Miniño, Arialdi M. "Mortality Among Teenagers Aged 12-19 Years: United States, 1999-2006." National Center for Health Statistics Data Brief Number 37. May 2010. https://www.cdc.gov/nchs/products/databriefs/db37.htm.

Montgomery, Charles. *The Happy City: Transforming Our Lives Through Urban Design*. New York: Farrar, Straus and Giroux, 2013.

Moskowwitz, Peter. *How to Kill a City: Gentrification, Inequality, and the Fight for the Neighborhood*. New York: Nation Books, 2017.

National Highway and Traffic Safety Administration, Fatality and Accident Research Database: www.nhtsa.gov/FARS.

Newbigin, Lesslie. "The Role of the Parish in Society." In *The Good Shepherd: Meditations on Christian Ministry in Today's World*, 85-90. Grand Rapids: Eerdmans, 1977.

Oldenburg, Ray. *The Great Good Place: Cafes, Coffee Shops, Community Centers, Beauty Parlors, General Stores, Bars, Hangouts, and How They Get You Through the Day*. New York: Marlowe and Company, 1999.

Owen, David. *Green Metropolis: Why Living Smaller, Living Closer, and Driving Less are the Keys to Sustainability*. New York: Riverhead, 2009.

Plantinga, Cornelius, Jr. *Engaging God's World: A Reformed Vision of Faith, Learning, and Living*. Grand Rapids: Eerdmans, 2002.

Pucher, John, and Ralph Buehler. "Cycling for Everyone: Lessons from Europe." *Transportation Research Record: Journal of the transportation research board* 2074 (2008): 58-65.

_____. "Cycling to Sustainability in Amsterdam." *Sustain*, 21 (Fall/Winter 2010): 36-41

Putnam, Robert D. *Bowling Alone: The Collapse and Revival of American Community*. New York: Simon and Schuster, 2000.

Reeves, Richard V. *Dream Hoarders: How the American Upper Middle Class is Leaving Everyone Else in the Dust, Why That is a Problem, and What to Do About It*. Washington, DC: Brookings Institution Press, 2017.

Robinson, Todd E. *A City within a City: The Black Freedom Struggle in Grand Rapids, Michigan*. Philadelphia: Temple University Press, 2013.

Rothstein, Richard. *The Color of Law: A Forgotten History of How Our Government Segregated America*. New York: Liverlight Publishing Company, 2017.

Snell, Bradford, U.S. Counsel. "American Ground Transport." In Part 4A of Hearings in S. 1167, the Industrial Reorganization Act, before the Subcommittee on Antitrust and Monopoly of the Committee of the Judiciary, U.S. Senate, 93rd Congress, 2nd Session. Washington, DC, 1974.

Sparks, Paul, Tim Soerens, and Dwight Friesen. *The New Parish: How Neighborhood Churches are Transforming Mission, Discipleship, and Community*. Downers Grove, IL: InterVarsity, 2014.

Speck, Jeff. *Walkable City: How Downtown Can Save America, One Step at a Time*. New York: Farrar, Straus and Giroux, 2012.

Stepp, Erin. "Annual Cost to Own and Operate a Motor Vehicle Falls to

$8,698, Finds AAA." April 28, 2015. http://newsroom.aaa.com/2015/04/annual-cost-operate-vehicle-falls-8698-finds-aaa-archive/.

Swope, Christopher. "Public Officials of the Year: Joseph P. Riley, Jr., Mayor, Charleston, South Carolina." *Governing Magazine.* 2003. http://www.governing.com/poy/Joseph-Riley.html.

Toly, Noah J. *Cities of Tomorrow and the City to Come: A Theology of Urban Life.* Grand Rapids, MI: Zondervan, 2015.

Trowbridge, M. J., and N. C. McDonald. "Urban Sprawl and Miles Driven Daily by Teenagers in the United States." *American Journal of Preventative Medicine* 34, no. 3 (March, 2008): 202-6.

True City, Hamilton, "Vision." 2017. http://truecityhamilton.ca/about/vision/.

Um, Stephen T., and Justin Buzzard. *Why Cities Matter.* Wheaton, IL: Crossway, 2011.

U. S. Department of Transportation, Bureau of Transportations Statistics. *Highlights of the 2001 National Household Travel Survey.* Washington DC, 2003.

U. S. Department of Transportation, Federal Highway Administration. A. Santos, N. McGuckin, H. Y. Nakamoto, D. Gray, and S. Liss. "Summary of Travel Trends: 2009 National Household Travel Survey." http://nhts.ornl.gov/2009/pub/stt.pdf.

U. S. Department of Transportation, Research and Innovative Technology Administration. "Transportation Vision for 2030: Ensuring personal freedom and economic vitality for a nation on the move." January 2008. https://www.rita.dot.gov/sites/default/files/rita_archives/rita_publications/transportation_vision_2030/pdf/entire.pdf.

U. S. Environmental Protection Agency (EPA), "Atlantic Station (Atlantic Steel Site Rehabilitation Project)." n.d. https://www.epa.gov/smartgrowth/atlantic-station-atlantic-steel-site-redevelopment-project.

_____. "Greenhouse Gas Emissions from a Typical Passenger Vehicle." May 2014. https://www.epa.gov/sites/production/files/2016-02/documents/420f14040a.pdf.

Verghese, Abraham. *Cutting for Stone.* New York: Random House, 2009.

Walker, Jarrett. *Human Transit: How Clear Thinking about Public Transit can Enrich our Communities and Lives.* Washington, DC: Island Press, 2011.

Walsh, Bryan. "How Green is Your Neighborhood?" *Time.* December 19,

2007. http://content.time.com/time/health/article/0,8599,1696857,00. html.

Wilberforce, William. *A Practical View of the Prevailing Religious System of Professed Christians, in the Higher and Middle Classes of this Country, Contrasted with Real Christianity.* 11th ed. London: Cadell and Davies, 1815.

Wilford, Justin. *Sacred Subdivisions: The Postsuburban Transformation of American Evangelicalism.* New York: New York University Press, 2012.

Williamson, Thad. *Sprawl, Justice, and Citizenship: The Civic Cost of the American Way of Life.* Oxford: Oxford University Press, 2010.

Index

Subject Index

Name Index

Printed in the USA
CPSIA information can be obtained
at www.ICGtesting.com
LVHW052033070923
757184LV00015B/927